CREATIVE SEXUALITY

Memoirs of a Catholic Nun

Barbaralie Stiefermann, OSF

Printed by CreateSpace, An Amazon.com Company

Available from Amazon.com, CreateSpace.com, and other retail outlets
Available on Kindle and online stores

About the cover:
Design by Dolores Garm
Black and white photos courtesy
of the School Sisters of St. Francis Archives
and
Golden autumn in forest © Olha Rohulya, lifedancephotography.net
Photo available from Dreamstime.com

Acknowledgements

I am grateful to our U.S. Provincials: Sisters Carol Rigali, Marilyn Ketteler, and Deborah Fumagalli for their encouragement and support. I express special thanks to Sister Mary Daniel for putting my handwritten manuscript on the computer. To Dolores Garm, I am indebted for graphic services and the cover design. Sister Agnes Marie Henkel deserves a debt of gratitude for her insights and editing skills. To Patricia Obletz, former staff writer of *Seventeen* magazine, I say "thank you" for also editing my manuscript. Melissa Wilson and Nancy Clark deserve special thanks for their advice on publishing and marketing.

I am indebted to Sister Mary Ann Eichenseer, archivist for the School Sisters of St. Francis Archives, for photos, and also Our Lady Help of Christians Parish, Frankenstein, Missouri.

I owe special thanks to Archbishop Rembert G. Weakland who graciously read the entire manuscript and offered invaluable advice.

This book was made possible through the generosity of Mark Sawko, Class of 1975, a student of mine at St. Francis High School in Wheaton, Illinois.

It takes a village to publish a book!

A wise person once said, "Gratitude is the memory of the heart." Memories have enriched my life. I choose to review and share my memory bank with you, the readers. I am grateful to the loved ones who have helped shape me and the experiences that have brought me great joy, fulfillment, and even sorrow at times. My memories of good times and good people reveal the light of Spirit that shines unceasingly on and in us all. May the "Good News" be proclaimed in and by our lives.

As author, I take full responsibility for what I have written. The topics, issues, opinions and insights do not necessarily reflect those of my religious community.

Introduction

I know all who read this book are wondering why a sister, a celibate, would dare write her memoirs in praise of human sexuality when so much of our Jansenistic and Catholic backgrounds have suppressed sexuality for centuries. Throughout Catholic history, the Church's teaching on sexual morality was summarized in Canon Law in 1917: "the primary purpose of marriage is the procreation and education of children. The secondary purpose is mutual support and remedy for concupiscence." The new Code of 1983 states the following: "The matrimonial covenant...is ordered by its nature to the good of the spouses and the procreation and education of offspring...." (C. 1055)

Vatican II deliberately rejected the priority of the procreative over the unitive end of marriage. The 1975 Vatican Declaration on sexual ethics went even further by identifying human sexuality in the unmarried as "the source of a person's most fundamental characteristics and as a crucial element leading to personal maturity and integration into society." Wholesome human sexuality fosters creative growth toward integration.

A study, *Human Sexuality*, commissioned by The Catholic Theological Society of America, published in 1979, states the following:

> It can be said that sexuality serves the development of human persons by calling them to constant creativity, that is to full openness to being, to the realization of every potential within the personality, to a continual discovery and expression of authentic selfhood. Procreation is one form of this call to creativity but by no means is it the only reason for sexual expression.

Sexuality assists in the development of genuine personhood by calling us to a clearer recognition of our relational nature, of our absolute need to reach out and embrace others in order to achieve personal fulfillment. Isn't the Creator ingenious by calling us constantly out of ourselves into relationship with others?

In gifting us with sexuality, the Creator showed no partiality. Every man and woman, young and old, regardless of race, class, ethnicity, and creed has this precious, creative gift. Someone once asked: "Did God make a mistake in giving everybody this gift?" Sex permeates life and influences every aspect of behavior, whether for good or evil.

Unfortunately, this gift is often misused and abused. Sex is the greatest gift to humanity, and yet, the greatest enigma. While it is a singular joy for all beings, it is also an enigma in its destructive potential for people and their relationships. It comes as no surprise then, that sex is one of the most difficult aspects of life, and the integration of sex with religion especially, compounds the complexity.

In a sex-saturated culture, I'm sure most readers of this book think that chastity is the ultimate nonconformity. On occasion, young men and women have asked me, "How do you live without sex? It's so much a part of who we are." True, it is definitely a part of who we are. But the question itself limits the understanding of human sexuality to the genital and generative, rather than as a force that permeates, influences, and affects every act of a person's being at every moment of existence. Sexuality is not operative in one restricted area of life. Rather, it is at the core and center of our total life-response. The movies, soap operas, reality TV, billboards, advertisements bombard us with "sex appeal." The sales of Viagra and Cialis keep increasing despite the warnings of serious side effects. Is it any wonder that our view of human sexuality is so limited?

As a sister, I feel as if I am going counter clockwise to the obsession of sex in American culture. Adultery abounds and appears to be acceptable behavior. Children in elementary school are already sexually active. Children are born out of wedlock. How do our young people learn to say "no" to prevailing pressures? Who and where are the models for these young people? How do any of us say "no" many times in our lives for a better "yes?"

As the battles ensue over same-sex marriage, the morning after pill, sex trafficking and sexual misconduct, I offer a different choice in life. Not all people are called to be celibates, but I venture to say that practicing chastity at various stages in anyone's life is strongly recommended. Think about it. Life would be different for many women and men had they chosen to remain chaste at certain phases in life. This gives individuals time and space to delve more deeply into themselves and to enhance their own personal development. This lays the foundation for developing strong and enduring relationships.

In reading my memoirs, I hope you will see that I have had a happy, fulfilling and rewarding life as a chaste celibate. I have had significant relationships with men and women. I have traveled; I am educated; I had the freedom to pursue my dreams and goals in life. I have had the flexibility to devote my life to others. Even though I have not given physical birth, I have given life and even restored life to many students with 36 years of teaching, 11 years as a campus minister, and 11 years as director of Alfons Art Gallery.

I am not a prude, I value my sexuality and this temple I call my body. I like what poet and farmer Wendell Berry had to say:

> You cannot devalue the body and value the soul—or value anything else. The isolation of the body sets it into direct conflict with everything in Creation. Nothing could be more absurd than to despise the body and yet yearn for its resurrection.

My successes and accomplishments in life can be attributed to the God-given creative energy of my sexuality. Starhawk, American writer and activist, said it well:

> Sex is the manifestation of the driving life force of the universe. Sexuality is an expression of the moving force that underlies everything and gives it life.

For those of you who read this book with the expectation that it is saturated with sexuality, you may be disappointed. This is not meant to be a study of the sociological and cultural factors which exert a cunning but powerful impact on the sexual mores of people. It is not a psychological study or a moral evaluation of sexual conduct. I merely want to broaden the traditional teaching of the purpose of sexuality; namely, "procreative and unitive to creative and integrative" no matter what our walk in life. I hope my life as a celibate subtly and implicitly exemplifies the integrative and creative sexual energies as seen through my relationships and experiences portrayed in my memoirs. Without minimizing the procreative and unitive, I invite you, the reader, to see human sexuality through a wider lens and value this precious gift. To the Christian and as a sister, it transcends the temporal and becomes sacramental. "Love one another as I love you."

Table of Contents

Chapter 1
Family Life on the Farm

In the spring when Mother Earth dons the fashions of greenery, buds and blossoms, I was born in my parental home in Frankenstein, Missouri, to August and Gertrude Stiefermann.

Yes, there really is a place called Frankenstein, which has no connection to the "flying monsters" of 1999. One hundred fifty years ago, the town was not named for the fictional mad scientist. People laugh and think I'm joking when I tell them I am from Frankenstein. Allow me to acquaint you with this beautiful hamlet in the foothills of the Ozarks, which has been a significant part of my life.

Frankenstein was settled by German immigrants during the 1860s. In 1863, the bloodiest year of the Civil War, when our country was encountering death, "Maria Hilf" (Mary Help) was coming to life, later to be known as Our Lady Help of Christians Catholic Church. Frankenstein's history is inseparable from the history of the church, parish, and school, known as St. Mary's.

One of the most influential and colorful priests to serve "Maria Hilf" parish was Father John Bachmeier, a native of Hofstetten, Bavaria, who arrived in 1889. It was he who initiated a discussion among parishioners about moving the church to a more suitable location where a town could be built. According to local tradition, he assisted the landowners and parishioners in clearing the land and building the new structure.

Father Bachmeier named the town "Frankenstein." There are at least two explanations of why he chose that name: to honor Gottfried Franken who had donated land for the second "Maria Hilf" site; to honor a German benefactor by that name who sent money to help establish the new community. The latter is the more widely accepted explanation.

In 1890, parishioners of "St. Mary's" congregation began to raise money to build a school that would also house a church on the second floor. As part of that fundraising effort, parishioners held a church picnic, beginning an annual tradition that still continues to this day. In addition to the good food, one of the great attractions is the beautiful quilts made by the women of the parish.

From the beginning, the parish picnic was a great community

effort in which young and old were enlisted to help. This event brings back many childhood memories. My mother made special dresses for me to wear for this occasion. Virtually the entire community halted other work on Friday and Saturday before the Sunday picnic to prepare for the event and returned the day after the picnic to complete the clean-up.

Church / school after new gable roof was added.

Construction of the church/school began in 1891. Built from massive stone blocks quarried

Father Alphonse Nicolas

a mile away, the two story hip-roofed structure featured a full finished basement. Later a new gable roof was added. The first floor had four classrooms, bisected by a hallway with two rooms on each side. A wide stairway in the center of the hallway led to a second floor which housed the church. This building, the third structure erected by and for the parishioners of "Maria Hilf," was completed in 1892, at a cost of $9,000. It was in this rock school which no longer housed the church, that I would attend first grade in 1938.

In 1963, the stone structure that once served as a church, rectory, school and convent, was razed. In retrospect, it saddens me that this historical building was not preserved.

Father Alphonse Nicolas, a native of Manchester in St. Louis County, arrived at Our Lady Help of Christians Parish in 1913. This was at the time the parish's population had grown considerably. In order to accommodate the growing parish, Father Nicolas

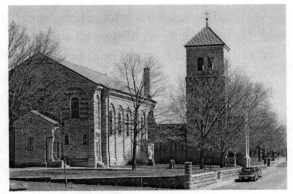

Our Lady Help of Christians Church
Photo courtesy: Kevin Muenks,
Edgewood Photography

2

made plans to build a new church. This remarkable priest could not have known it at the time that he was destined to become the parish's longest serving pastor, presiding from 1913-1932 and again from 1936-1943. He was a great friend of my grandfather and my parents and often visited our home.

By 1921, Father Nicolas had a sufficient amount of money to begin the construction of the church. A building committee was elected by parishioners. A contract was entered into with the renowned German-American architectural firm of Ludewig and Dreisvoerner of St. Louis.

Tony Gabelsberger, a native of Dingolfing, Bavaria, was named the head stone mason. Among the tedious, backbreaking jobs was the hauling of thousands of cubic yards of stone, blasted out of a hillside of one of the parishioner's farm. The quarried stone was hauled by teams of horses and mules, pulling wagons up a long hill. My dad, a young man at the time, recalled that he could haul only one stone at a time on the wagon.

A current photo of the interior of the church showing changes implemented after Vatican II

The church was dedicated on Labor Day, September 1, 1923, a fitting day since so much volunteer labor was involved in this new edifice. My grandfather built the pews for the chapel which was used in the winter to conserve heat. The area newspaper *Unterrified Democrat* reported, "The cash outlay for the building was less than $30,000"owing largely to the generous contributions of labor and material by the parishioners, a credit not only to the Frankenstein parish, but to the whole county, being one of the finest buildings erected in the county for many years."

In July 2013, I had the good fortune to attend the Sesquicentennial Celebration in Frankenstein where much of my family history is woven throughout the decades. To commemorate the occasion, the parish published a 656 page volume entitled *Frankenstein,*

A Thoroughly Catholic Settlement: from Maria Hilf to Our Lady Help of Christians, 1863–2013, from which I derived the history for my memoirs. The celebration was one of the epiphanies in my life as I journeyed back to my roots.

Historian, Gary Kremer, a native of Frankenstein, and executive director of the State Historical Society of Missouri, said "Early Frankenstein residents were incredibly resilient and self-reliant people, whose lives were focused inward, toward themselves and each other, bound together in a faith community that shared common beliefs, traditions and practices."

Thus, to quote Mark Twain: "All that goes to make the me in me began in a Missouri village…" called Frankenstein. On April 27, 1932, Dr. Herman Gove, our family physician, welcomed me into the world at 2:30 a.m. My mother had a difficult time giving birth and was advised not to have any more children. When I left the security of her womb and entered life, I was near death. Dr. Gove told my father that if he wanted me to be baptized, he had better do so immediately. Without hesitation, my dad baptized me. In tears, he then went to my Grandma Stiefermann who lived with us and was eagerly awaiting the news of a "boy or girl." Upon hearing that in all probability I would not live, Grandma consoled my dad with the words: "Don't worry, August. She will live and someday be the nun in your family." This was a secret my dad carried in his heart for many years.

Contrary to the advice of her doctor, Mom gave birth to six girls and one son, all of whom were born at home, except the last daughter, Rosemarie. She was born at St. Mary's Hospital in Jefferson City on December 21, 1942, and died three days later. My sister Margaret and I carried the little white coffin to the parish cemetery in a private ceremony on Christmas Eve. As Christians were about to celebrate the birth of Christ, we, as a family, were experiencing the death of a child born to eternal life. I am grateful that Mom risked having more children. Growing up the second oldest child with four sisters, Margaret, Betty, Theresa and Kathleen, and one brother, Charles, was a blessing. At an early age I learned to live in community. We learned to share; to be concerned about each other. In spite of our arguments and childhood fights, we had a deep sense of loyalty to one another. No one dared to say an unkind remark about any of our siblings. I learned to defend myself and to uphold what is right and just.

I value the open spaces and freedom I had growing up on a farm. As children, we benefitted greatly by the German culture Grandpa Frank Stiefermann had established. Although Grandpa had died before I was born, his presence was still alive among us. As a result of his hard work, we had an apple orchard, vineyard, bee hives, pecan, hickory and walnut trees, fruit trees, vegetable garden, and even a persimmon tree. Grandma nurtured a variety of flowers and roses in our yard that were often placed on the altars in our parish church.

August and Gertrude Stiefermann Family
Back: August, Gertrude
Middle: Barbaralie, Bertha Marie "Betty," Margaret
Front: Theresa, Charles, Kathleen (circa 1940)

Grandpa, an artisan, built our house in 1896. (The fourth generation of the family now lives in this home.) The rooms were large with high ceilings, stenciled borders on the walls, and a decorative circle in the middle of the ceilings. Wainscoting in the kitchen and dining room was an attractive feature that set them apart as special.

Stiefermann home where I was born and raised

Along with his five sons and three daughters, Grandpa formed the Stiefermann Dance Band. In one of the rooms upstairs, the people in the community gathered to "promenade left and promenade right." It was at one of these dances that my mother, who spoke only English, met my father. "The Waltz You Saved for Me," sparked the beginning of their relationship.

My grandmother, Elizabeth, taught simple prayers to me when I was only three years old. As I was kneeling by her side one morning, she had a heart attack and died. I gazed at her lying on the hardwood floor in the dining room. I thought she had fallen asleep. I shook her and said, "Grandma, wake up! Wake up." Upon hearing this, my mother, who was in the kitchen, came quickly to the scene. She pulled me away from Grandma and said in a muted voice, "Grandma is dead." This was my first experience of death.

Grandma was laid out in our parlor and many people came to pay their last respects. This left a lasting impression upon me. Isn't it interesting that she who had predicted I would some day be a nun,

Frank and Elizabeth (Backes) Stiefermann Family
Back: John, Theresa, Gertrude, August, Rudolph;
Front: Raymond, Frank, Ernest, Elizabeth, Agnes

died with only her little grandchild kneeling at her side.

I soon learned that the farm provided many life and death experiences. I saw sexuality manifested at an early age in the breeding and birthing process of animals. I also witnessed and marveled at the

Barbaralie, age 3

nurturing of animals toward their offspring. Calves, colts, and litters of pigs were born. Some of the animals and fowl were butchered and many were shipped to market. As a child, I learned to let go of my favorite animals. It was in my youth that I acquired a great love of horses and saw "Tom" become old, disabled and die. A saddle without a horse was just one more experience of death to me.

The farm provided numerous opportunities for excitement and responsibility. We each had our chores and were held accountable. There were times we moaned and groaned about plucking bugs off the potato leaves (pesticides were not used), and picking blackberries and gooseberries when we wanted to play. Work was a developmental process in helping us grow up and learn skills for later life.

In a rural environment, there were no limits to the use of our imaginations. We improvised our own games. We played church, school, hospital, house. Playing house with my sisters Margaret and Betty

6

evoked competition like no other. We each decorated and arranged our little abode under a tree and argued who had the best. Of course, there was no objectivity in our judging. Is it any wonder that later in life our homes expressed the finesse of interior decorators who at times are still in competition.

Harvesting corn, filling silo, hauling hay, molasses and wine-making were fascinating experiences few children have today. Most of these activities required hired men to help my dad. He did not allow his wife and five girls to work in the fields. We girls helped Mom prepare the lavish dinners on special occasions.

The work ethic of the German nationality was certainly manifested in my dad. He was an advocate for the University of Missouri Extension Service. He relied heavily on advice from the Osage County agent to improve farming practices during the 1940s. In later years, he often related how their advice helped him to become a highly successful farmer.

He worked for the USA Agricultural Stabilization program in the 1930s to the 1960s, initially doing farm crop and acreage

My dad circa age 27

compliance measurement surveys, and later, was an elected Agricultural Stabilization Compliance Surveys (ASES) county committeeman.

During the 1930s and 1940s, Daddy was a trustee of the parish. He was president of St. Mary's School Board in the late 1940s when the high school was a public school taught by the School Sisters of St.

Francis. In 1950, St. Mary's High School closed and students transferred to St. Joseph School in Westphalia, which was the interim R-3 School District High School, while the new Fatima High School was being constructed. (My sister Betty won the contest for naming the high school). Daddy was a founding member of the R-3 School District Board. It's amazing that my dad, who had only four years of grade school, was a strong advocate of education as demonstrated by all his

Daddy, circa age 23

six children attending college and his dedicated service to St. Mary's School and the R-3 School District.

Daddy was a kind, gentle, soft-spoken, wise man who could be moved to tears upon hearing a poignant story, a stirring musical composition, a theatrical performance. He was disciplined, organized, serious, intelligent. Above all, he was a holy man who sought time for prayer and solace. He had great devotion to Our Lady of Perpetual Help, and attended services every Tuesday evening at Our Lady Help of Christians Church. Years later, pastor Monsignor William Fischer said to me, "Your dad is a saint."

Mom, circa age 25, with a marcel hairstyle

On June 24, 1930, at age 33, Daddy married my mother who was 26. They enjoyed 59 years of conjugal love. At that time, it was unusual to marry that late in life. I attribute the security in our family to the maturity of both my parents. I was blessed to have the upbringing by parents who had their "act together," especially during the Depression years.

Before my mother married, she had worked as a maid and nanny for the Siegels, a wealthy family in St. Louis who had one child, Mary Louise. This exposure to wealthy people, among other things, taught her fine dining. Contrary to family life today, the dining room was the most important room in our home. We learned how to properly set a table, serve food from the left and remove dishes from the right. "And don't put candles on the table if you don't intend to light them," I can still hear Mom say. She spent hours ironing linen tablecloths and napkins and was happy for fabrics later developed when ironing was done only as a "touch up."

Mom was a capricious, spontaneous woman who had a flair

Marriage of Mom and Daddy, June 24, 1930

8

for fashion and beauty. The Irish in her was a great complement to the German in my dad. When a rainbow arched across the sky, she gathered us all together to behold this prismatic wonder. Many summer nights we sat on the front porch gazing at the moon and a star-spangled sky as Mom made up stories about the "man in the moon" and the Big Dipper.

When the radio played lively music, she would grab a dish towel and do a scarf dance around the dining room table. Fortunately, or unfortunately, whoever happened to be in the room at this time had to engage in a free-style dance with her.

Mom never had piano lessons, but one would think she was a virtuoso as she sat on the bench and played familiar tunes with lots of clash, discord and distortion, and yet, we were still able to discern the song she was playing. My brothers-in-law, and later, their children, considered her piano playing sheer entertainment.

The sturdy rocking chair that Mom sat in and rocked us to sleep is an heirloom in the family. How well I remember her beautiful coloratura voice as she sang Brahms' "Lullaby" that lured us to sleep. She knew every church hymn and popular song of the time and spent many of her working hours singing. People who heard her said she should have been an opera singer.

Joseph and Margaret (Walsh) Koenigsfeld Family
Back: Anna, Joseph, Barbara, Mary "Mamie," Gertrude
Front: Joseph, Fred, Margaret

Every night we prayed the family rosary around the dining room table. Father Patrick Peyton's slogan, "The family that prays together stays together" was quoted often by my parents. The Litany of the Blessed Virgin, which Mom knew by memory, followed the rosary. If something struck us as funny, it was sure to happen during the rosary, and we tried our best to suppress our giggles.

Sundays were truly a day of rest for us. Working on the farm was unheard of. Shopping malls were non-existent; stores were closed.

Every Sunday we went to Mass dressed in our finest clothes. When we arrived home, we changed into more casual attire. In our family, strong distinctions were made regarding clothing: Sunday clothes, school and work, and we dared not interchange them. The ritual of changing clothes to suit the occasion is a discipline we learned and still practice.

Our greatest joy was visiting Grandma Margaret and Grandpa Joseph Koenigsfeld every Sunday afternoon. Grandpa raised sheep on his hillside farm. Because we did not have these wooly animals on our farm, they fascinated us. Feeding the lambs, sheering the sheep, washing and cording the wool to put in comforters were learning experiences. I enjoyed hearing the "baa baa" of sheep and the "cock-a-doodle-do" of a rooster on Grandpa's farm.

Often our cousins, who were our ages, came to visit our mutual grandparents. What fun we had playing "no laughing, no talking, no moving red light," as we ran and abruptly stopped on "red light," and dared not move or we had to start from the beginning.

After the physical exertion, we sat at a large rectangular table in Grandma's kitchen to an elaborate mid-afternoon lunch. Aunt Mamie, Mom's unmarried sister who lived with her parents, delighted in serving us homemade bread, butter and peachjack, a combination of molasses and cooked peaches. Both Grandma and Aunt Mamie could have won the Betty Crocker Award for their homemade pies and cakes made from scratch. They took great pride in their cooking and baking.

I fondly remember Grandma's beautiful smile and serene disposition as she sat in her rocking chair braiding her long gray hair which she wrapped around her head like a halo. Her family, the Walsh clan, was the storytellers, jokesters, and merrymakers. My great Uncle John Walsh was a marvelous storyteller who had no family or home of his own. He literally walked from family to family located in various towns and spent a week or two. Today one would think family and relatives would eventually tire of such a "free loader." This was not the case. When we saw him walking down the hill with a satchel on his back, we yelled, "Uncle John is coming" and ran out of the house to meet him half-way up the hill. He always received a warm welcome from us. We loved to listen to his stories, experiences, and news from all the neighboring towns. He was truly a storybook character who touched the lives of many people, especially our family.

Our aunts and uncles from my dad's side all spoke German

when they came to visit us. To this day I regret that I never learned German. Before and after World War II, we children wanted no part of that language. My dad, who lived to be a centenarian, lost all his family members and old friends with whom he had spoken German. It was

Daddy, circa age 83
Photo courtesy: Margaret E.
(Stiefermann) Powers

sad to hear him say near the end of his life, "I can't believe I have lost my native tongue." Had we children learned German, this would not have happened.

I also regret the vanishing of the family farm in our country. It is difficult to sustain and maintain a small farm today. Farming has become big business. Times have changed since Daddy tilled the land. My brother Charles had a full time job in the state as an engineer in the Department of Natural Resources (DNR) and farmed on the side. In reality, he had two full-time jobs. The same is true of his son Michael who is also an engineer. As a family, we are fortunate to still have the farm after all these years. I wish that children today would have the privilege and pleasure of growing up on a farm as I have had.

Something unheard of today because of economic factors, job changes and mobility in society—Daddy was born, lived, and died in Frankenstein at age 100 and four months; he was buried on the same plot of land. When the parish church needed a new cemetery, a portion of our farm land was chosen. It is a meditation to walk through the cemetery and see the resting place of the many people who were special in my life's pilgrimage. As St. John Chrysostom stated: "Those whom we love and lose are no longer where they were before. They are now wherever we are."

The term "human sexuality" was never in my parents' vocabulary as I was growing up. What was apparent were the models I had of wholesome sexuality manifested in loving, enduring relationships of my parents, grandparents, uncles and aunts. One thing was certain: my family and the other people in the village of Frankenstein, like Jesus, were in love with the birds, the fish, sheep, lilies of the field, the soil, sun and rain, the mustard seed. They shared a wholesome relationship with their creaturely brothers and sisters. As Wendell Berry states, "There is an uncanny resemblance between our behavior toward each other and our behavior toward the earth—between our relation to our sexuality and our relation to the reproductivity of the earth."

Chapter II
Attending St. Mary's School

I could not wait to attend St. Mary's School. Since there was no kindergarten, at age five I charged out of the house and followed my sister Margaret to her first grade class. Sister Oringa Stablo, a School Sister of St. Francis, thought I had had the permission of my parents to come to school. How proud I was to sit with the other students on little red chairs in front of the room for reading class. I grasped my primer firmly and held it upright as I was called upon to read. "Run, Jane, run. See Jane run."

Then to the utter dismay of everyone, my dad appeared in the doorway. Sister Oringa proceeded slowly to the door. I heard Daddy say, "I came to get Barbaralie; we did not know she had gone to school this morning." I blushed and felt a tremor in my legs. The whole class knew I was a fake first grader who had no business being in school. Sister gently took my hand and walked to the door with me. Daddy ushered me down the corridor, grasping my hand tightly. In a gentle voice he said "I'll get you a box of crayons, paper, and pencils, and you can have school at home with your younger sisters Betty and Theresa." Without a single reprimand, Daddy drove home and abandoned me at the yard gate. I stood on the front steps of our home and jumped up and down in protest as he drove off.

After this display of anger, and my mother ignoring me as she was sweeping the front porch, I had no choice but to resign myself to staying at home. Later in life, I reflected on this early experience and wondered why my mother and dad had not reprimanded me. Would this not have evoked a spanking or punishment from most parents at that time? In retrospect, I think it pleased them that I was so eager to learn.

An interesting feature of St. Mary's School is that it was a public school. In 1923, when the new church was completed, Father Nicolas led a successful effort to transform the parochial school into a public school. Thus, the Osage County taxpayers assumed the burden of the school's operating costs. For nearly three decades, the county also paid the salaries of the School Sisters of St. Francis who continued teaching at St. Mary's. Eventually, the school transferred from public to parochial in 1952, at which time the sisters continued to teach. The religion classes were held in the three storied bell-tower of the church, the chapel and priests' sacristy.

In second grade I recall the state inspectors coming to our school. Years later, the sisters told me it was a stressful time, when periodically the inspectors even checked their desks and removed holy cards they would give as rewards. Even though Catholic symbols were nowhere in sight, the young sisters stood before us as the greatest witnesses to Catholic education. The sisters, clad in full habit wore a crucifix and rosary. I saw this as a big contradiction. How could this be, I thought? We were not allowed to have a crucifix on the wall, yet the sisters were wearing a large cross.

Interestingly, Father Nicolas preached from the pulpit on Sundays that only Catholics could be saved. Unless I wasn't paying

Barbaralie, 4th grade

attention, I never heard the sisters teach this. Was it because there were Protestants in the school? How terrible it would have been for the Catholic children to condemn their non-Catholic classmates.

Father Nicolas came to our home and reprimanded my dad for attending the funeral services of our neighbor, who was not Catholic, and for taking me with him to the Baptist church. I fell asleep because I thought it was a boring service—no incense, candles, flowers, vestments, kneeling—just singing and preaching. To this day I cannot figure out how Father Nicolas found out that we had gone to this forbidden place.

And what was Daddy's response to our pastor? "Father, I disagree with you entirely on your thinking and treatment of non-Catholics. Doesn't the Bible say, "Love your neighbor?" Needless to say, Daddy and the pastor each held to his own belief; however, it is amazing it did not destroy their friendship. I am grateful that Daddy, who dealt with many people of other faith traditions, provided a role model for tolerance and acceptance of all religions. As a result of the guidance and teaching of my parents and the sisters, we developed a strong sense of right and wrong, a respect for all of creation, and an openness and tolerance of all people.

I distinctly felt I had achieved a new attribute called "conscience" when I was in third grade. I stole 50 cents from my dad's wallet. On a bright, sunny day, I walked to the town grocery store, which was a mile from our home. I delighted in choosing a large assortment of candies. In those days, 50 cents could buy lots of candy: gum drops, candy corn, licorice, chocolate, orange slices, jaw breakers, lollipops. I placed all of these on the counter and handed Mr. Jaeger two quarters. He looked at me suspiciously but refrained from questioning. "Enjoy your candy and have a good day," he said. I walked out of the store with my large acquisition and proceeded down the steps. By the time I reached the sidewalk, my conscience became fully awakened. Should I give the candy back to Mr. Jaeger? Should I take it home and share it with my family? Would my family suspect that I stole either the money or the candy?

As I walked down the graveled road, that bag became heavier and heavier. My conscience continued to wage war with me and finally won. On the outskirts of town, I marched over to a sycamore tree by the side of the road, and with a sigh of relief, placed the bag on the ground. Looking around and staking out my territory, I wanted to make sure no one else was traveling down this road. I began digging a hole with my bare hands. I dug and dug. It was tedious and even painful trying to dig a hole large and deep enough to accommodate all the candy. What an accomplishment it was to finally smooth the loose dirt over the candy, leaving no trace of my guilt feelings that had now been buried.

I strolled down the road toward home thinking how stupid it was to steal and to cover up, and what a price I had to pay. With my conscience still tormenting me, I entered the house feeling so guilty that everyone sensed there was something wrong.

"Where were you?" Margaret asked. "We've been looking for you." "You were gone a long time," Betty said as she accentuated the word "long." Plagued with questions and comments, I could only respond by remaining silent. Finally, when I was at the verge of tears, Daddy asked, "What is the matter?"

I cried. I confessed. All my siblings in unison said, "Where did you bury it? Let's dig it up! We can all eat the candy." My wise father said, "No, let it be buried." Thereafter, every time we drove past that sycamore tree, even for many years after I had become a sister, the memories and questions still surfaced. "Are lollipops growing under the tree? Are the gum drops in bloom yet?" Experiences such as this mold and shape character. I maintain that life is our greatest teacher and we never stop learning.

My third grade teacher, Sister Minerva, taught us how to play croquet during recess. At home my sisters and I improvised crude mallets, arcs and used walnuts and Osage oranges as balls. As a result of this practice at home, we became experts in playing croquet. By

Father Lawrence Rost

the time I was in seventh grade, I had no fear of challenging any adult to a game. Unbeknown to my classmates and me, our pastor, Father Lawrence Rost, peered from the rectory window one afternoon to watch us play. He saw that I had gone through all the arcs and did not hit the final stake, thus delaying the game and declaring myself the winner. Instead, I hit everyone else's ball and knocked them off course putting them even farther behind in the game. After I had my thrills and succeeded in hitting most of the other balls, I aimed and hit the stake and declared victory.

After school, Father Rost called me to the rectory. In his gentle manner he said to me, "I observed you playing croquet today, and I did not like what I saw. There is an undesirable trait in your character when you have no regard for others, who were already behind in the game, and by hitting and knocking their balls, they had no chance of winning. Imagine how they must have felt." At that moment, I felt ashamed yet justified, and replied "But I followed all the rules; I did not cheat." "I realize this is how croquet is played, but did you have to knock their balls making it even more difficult for them to win when you were already winning?" he questioned. "Is there not an element of selfishness, even cruelty in your behavior? Is there a lack of tolerance and disregard for the feelings of others?" Wow! Those were strong words to me. Was I being cruel, selfish, intolerant?

At the time, I thought our pastor was taking all the fun out of croquet—at least fun for me, the winner. It wasn't until later that I processed his admonition and realized what a true pastor he was in taking the time to instill Christian values and to assist me in growing up.

Often, Father Rost, as did many of the priests, came to our home and my mom fixed lavish meals that in all probability surpassed what their housekeepers would have made. The priests were always welcomed guests in our home. Thus, I was not fearful of the parish priests and felt at ease with them.

Father Nicolas, in his retiring years, lost his eyesight. He loved to go fishing in the Big Loose Creek by our home, as he had done in his younger days along with other priests from the Archdiocese of St. Louis. After my sister Betty dug the worms for bait, I sat on the banks with Father telling him when the cork had gone under and when to pull up to catch the fish. It gave me a good feeling to help him in his declining years. He had done so much for the parish and was greatly respected for his accomplishments, especially getting electricity in this rural area and building the church and faith community.

Already in seventh and eighth grades, I felt a strong attraction to boys and they toward me. I was assigned to clean the classroom after school with Gus. He chased me around the room with a broom, and it finally ended up in two pieces which we glued together and discreetly placed in the closet. The next morning, Sister Parillia Kerkmann held up the two pieces and asked, "Who did this?" Gus and I shamefully stood up before the class. I could tell that Sister was surprised that I was one of the culprits. In addition to having to buy a new broom, we had an additional week to clean under her supervision. Needless to say, Gus and I didn't have much fun that second week.

St. Mary's School was the social center of the parish. There was no theatre, bowling alley, ice-cream parlor or shops—just one store which became an institution and later burned and was deeply mourned by all. The young people had no place to "hang out." The youthful, vibrant sisters provided not only a good education, but recreation in many forms. The sisters conducted the 4-H Club, drama, music, nature walks and many other activities. Sister Adelaide Brickel taught soccer; Sister Chrysanthus Tellesen, two-part harmony. Many children forfeited taking the bus and chose to walk home from school just to listen to the suspense stories of Sister Abilia Webkes. Sister Conleth Clayton, who had a great sense of humor, managed to tame a squirrel that appeared on the nuns' doorstep every morning and entertained us with its antics. Sister Cyriaka Woida nursed a little goat with a broken leg that a student had brought to her. The sisters named the goat "Period" because of the black spot on her coat. As the sisters walked up and down the sidewalk praying, the pet goat followed them back and forth as if in deep prayer. I asked my dad several times to drive past the convent late afternoons just to see the sisters and Period praying.

Sister Cyriaka Woida feeding Period, the goat

It was the nuns who made high school graduation a spectacular event. Parents and students were amazed at the transformation of the hall in the old, rock school. Under dim lighting and a nostalgic setting, one small graduating class rowed across the stage in boats to the popular song, "Moonlight and Roses." Sister Felicia Lieser, principal, and the other sisters were the masterminds behind such memorable events. From picking walnuts and pecans, building a rock garden by the old convent, taking walks up and down the hills, the sisters were the "Flying Nuns" that generated new life in this rural parish.

Father Nicolas also contributed to our fun by purchasing large, colorful kites in St. Louis. On a March, windy day during recess, the whole school would gather and write wishes on small, square pieces of paper, puncture a hole in the middle and pull them through the string of the kite. It was thrilling to watch our wishes, propelled by the wind advance up to the kite flying high in the sky. And often our wishes came true.

During the winter after a snowfall, Fathers Nicolas and his associate, Anthony Talir hosed down the snow on the incline behind the school while we were in class. By the time recess occurred, the snow had frozen and the entire school had a skating party. The miracle is that none of us ever were injured, even though we had many falls.

I would be remiss if I did not mention the many processions that were held in our parish church. Mom braided our hair, dressed us in white and made sure we had enough rose petals in our baskets to strew before the Blessed Sacrament as we processed down the aisles. At times, we also held a bouquet of flowers and strewed petals. After such dramatic and impressionistic experiences, I came to know the Eucharist as something special and precious in our lives. Eucharistic celebrations in the faith community are still special to me, even though we no longer process and strew flowers.

During World War II, the students at St. Mary's gathered sacks of walnuts and often came to school with stained hands. The hulls were used to stain the army boys' pants. Also, many commodities were rationed during the war: shoes, sugar, flour, coffee, gas, etc. Father Nicolas gave my dad his shoe stamps in exchange for coffee. World War II opened my eyes to a much larger world than the small, insulated community of Frankenstein. The townspeople, especially my dad, began discussing and responding more to global issues.

Dozens of community boys, who had rarely been more than 100 miles from their homes, were now drafted into the military and served half way around the world. Their pictures were posted in the back of Our Lady Help of Christians Church. Many mothers whose sons were in the military came to Mass every day, often in tears if they had a son missing in action. I witnessed the anguish in their faces and felt sorry for them. The men came home as changed men after the war, and only one failed to return.

The backdrop to the war was the sisters who remained steadfast and focused in their efforts to provide us with an education that would benefit us for life no matter where we went in the world. They inspired, motivated and challenged us to a life beyond St. Mary's School. Is it any wonder that later Roy Scantlin, the State Superintendent of Schools in Missouri said to Daddy, "Those School Sisters of St. Francis are the best teachers in this State."

Celibacy was a term that was not in my vocabulary while I attended St. Mary's School; however, I knew sisters did not marry, as was the case also with the priests. Their lifestyle was appealing to me, as well as to others, and offered another option to marriage. They were happy and committed to the people they served.

The sisters offered another dimension that often captured my attention—community life. I could see they enjoyed living, working, and praying together. Their combined sexual energies had the power to birth us anew. As I now reflect on their lifestyle, they had the healthy humility to live close to the earth and the things of earth. Simple living. The irony was that these sisters were born and raised in cities like Chicago and Milwaukee and were able to adapt so well to a rural community.

Chapter III
Answering the Call

As I reflect on my call to religious life, I vividly remember the pain and struggle in responding. When I began hearing that call deep inside me, I did everything to smother the choice for a vocation to religious life. I paged through magazines looking at beautiful homes, interior designs, palatial gardens, planning my dream home. As I passed a bridal shop in Jefferson City, I imagined myself in an elegant gown displayed in the window. As you can see, I had other plans for my life.

One afternoon, Father Rost, the pastor who had summoned me to the rectory because he did not like the way I played the game of croquet, requested my appearance again. I had changed my manner of playing croquet so I could only assume that he might want to give me a letter for my dad since he was president of the high school board and a trustee of the parish. Often my sisters and I were messengers for the pastor.

To my utter surprise, there was no letter. Father led me into the parlor and asked me to be seated. An uncomfortable silence ensued. Then in a prophetic voice, he said, "Barbaralie, I think God is calling you to religious life." This statement absolutely terrified me. It was as if God verbalized what I had been trying to suppress in my mind for months.

I solemnly rose to my feet, walked over to the large picture window, turned my back to the pastor, and with folded arms peered outside at a poetic snowfall. Finally in a quivering voice, I said, "Father, even if God is calling me, I will not answer."

There was a long dramatic silence. And in his same prophetic, calm voice, he said, "What does it profit a man if he gain the whole world and suffer the loss of his soul?"

My very soul shrieked! I felt as if someone had pushed me down an elevator shaft and I had hit a cement bottom. Silence and darkness reigned. When I managed to gain my equilibrium, I turned and asked Father, "Is this all you want to say to me?" And he said, "Yes." "Thank you, Father," was my reply as I opened the rectory door and walked down the steps on heavy feet and with a pounding heart. From that day on, the "Hound of Heaven" pursued me. I was out of breath, most of the time trying to run away from myself and from God. I was empty. I was lonesome. I was sad. It seemed as if everywhere I went, I faced a dead-end street.

After three months of agony, I finally rang the rectory doorbell without being summoned by the pastor. Father came to the door with a big smile and invited me in. "Father, you're right. I can't keep running away. If I am to be happy, I must answer God's call," I said.

He saw that I was on the verge of tears, gently placed his arm on my shoulder and led me to his office. After I was seated, he pulled from the shelf a *Directory of Religious Communities* throughout the United States. He began paging through the book and said, "It's important that you enter the community that is best suited for you. Besides having a religious vocation, you also have a call to a specific religious order." There was no thought in my mind of entering an order other than the School Sisters of St. Francis who had taught me, but I allowed him to proceed with his search.

As we looked at various orders, I was appalled at some of the strange religious habits and thought—no way! He finally came to a page and stopped abruptly. "Maybe you would like to become a Little Sister of the Poor." I thought he was being serious and emphatically said, "No, I'm not going to spend my life begging." He burst out in laughter. He must have known that he would get a strong reaction from me. "It appears you've already made up your mind," he said. "Yes, I know the School Sisters of St. Francis community is right for me," I replied. Father confirmed my decision. He, too, had great love and respect for these Franciscan sisters.

After leaving the rectory that afternoon, I felt relieved in knowing that I had made the decision to become a sister, but getting parental consent, and making the preparations placed another burden on me. The thought of leaving home already created tremendous anxiety within me. That same day, I asked Mom if I may become a sister. I could tell by the look on her face that she was somewhat surprised and not too happy about the request. I would be the first to leave the nest even before my older sister. Mom said, with a bit of sadness in her voice, "Whatever is best for you is what I want, but you need to ask your dad. I think you are too young to make such a decision."

I met Sister Cyriaka after school and told her of my plans. She was elated and said she would get the list of what I needed to bring and assist me in preparing for this event in my life. She also told me to let

Sister Felicia Lieser, the principal, know.

Late that same day, I met Daddy at the yard gate as he was returning home from his office in Linn. When I asked him if I may become a sister, he looked at me and said "no" in an unconvincing tone of voice. I'll admit this was not the best time to approach my dad. Consequently, there was no discussion. However, I knew I had to persist and let him know this was not a whimsical fantasy of mine.

One week later, I approached him and asked again with the certitude that he would say yes this time. The answer was "no" and nothing more was said. This made me feel uncomfortable because time was running out. The month of August was the acceptable time to enter the convent. I managed to strengthen my determination. If I received another no, then that would be a sure sign that God was not calling me.

For the third time, I asked, "Daddy, may I go to the convent?" He looked at me intently and gave no response this time and slowly walked away. Looking back I think he must have reflected on his mother's own words at my birth, which I had no knowledge of when I made my request.

Ah, I thought—silence is consent! I lost no time in purchasing the items necessary and started to pack my dad's small antique trunk. Black and white colors predominated: black shoes, black stockings, black garb, white collar. What a contrast to what I had been wearing! And, of course, Daddy was quietly paying the bills behind the scenes.

No words can describe my internal turbulence as the time drew nearer. Two classmates, Gus and Louis, heard the news and took bets that I would not stay in the convent. Our neighbors, Leonard and Dell Burchard, who were not Catholic, were stunned and raised objections when I took their mail to them, which was a daily routine for my sisters and me. I felt as if no one was on my side. I prayed and prayed. O God, give me strength and courage. I felt stronger and more determined in my intent.

Mom and I purchased a one-way train ticket to Milwaukee, Wisconsin. Three things struck me as I stood trembling with her at the ticket counter. 1) Mom is only buying a one-way ticket. What if I don't like it in the convent? 2) I'm going to Wisconsin to a place I have never been or even seen a photo of. What will it be like to go from the farm to a city? 3) The sisters at St. Joseph Convent have never seen me. What if they don't like me? Then what? I calmed myself by reasoning if God is

22

calling me as Father Rost insisted, then God must know what is right for me.

Several days before leaving, I took a train ride to Jefferson City. Because it was shadowed by fear and anxiety, I have no recollection of who went with me, if anyone, or why I went. Was this to be a last fling? What I do remember is a policeman walking up to me saying, "You have just jay-walked, so I will have to issue you a ticket."

I didn't even realize Jefferson City had such a law. I saw nothing wrong with taking a shortcut when the street was clear of traffic. I paid the fine of $4.00. I was relieved to know I had a ticket to get home, since I had only a few coins left in my purse to buy an ice-cream cone at Central Dairy, where Daddy had often taken us. What should have been an inspirational train ride home with beautiful scenery along the Missouri River was a lonely, bleak and barren journey that seemed to go nowhere. All I could think of was the long train ride I would soon take to Milwaukee.

The next day Father Rost invited me to the rectory after Mass for breakfast. The first question he asked was "Did your dad give his consent to your going to the convent?" I did not let him know that I was operating on the premise that silence was consent. I firmly answered, "Yes, he did."

At that precise moment, Kate the housekeeper, placed an egg sunnyside up in front of me. I never eat eggs because I have such a dislike for them. The smell of the sulphur was enough to anesthetize me, to say nothing of the yolk that swirled on my plate after I put my fork into it. How will I ever get that egg down without gagging and even vomiting? Even more so, how will I avoid embarrassing Father and Kate? The conversation was sparse. He must have sensed that something was wrong when he asked, "Are you getting nervous that you will soon be leaving?" I responded, "I am very nervous" as I took another gulp and flushed the remaining egg down with orange juice. I couldn't believe I ate the whole thing!

When I returned home, Mom asked, "What did Kate serve for breakfast?"

"You aren't going to believe that I ate an egg sunnyside up," was my reply.

My mother was furious. "To think I've worked all these years to get you to eat an egg. I've creamed eggs, scrambled, deviled, colored

23

eggs and disguised them with other foods, and now you tell me you ate an egg sunnyside up!"

What could I say? "I'm sorry, Mom," was my pathetic response.

Several times as I was making preparations to go to the convent, Mom said to me, "You are going to be sent home for refusing to eat eggs. In the convent, you'll have to eat everything set before you." Actually, she was right. The director of novices checked our tables to make sure the boiled eggs were all gone from the bowl, but I had worked out a deal with the sisters sitting near me who loved eggs.

Years later when the flu shot was initiated, I broke out in a rash all over my body and became seriously ill. The doctor said to me, "I wish you had told me about your dislike of eggs. That was Nature's way of protecting you. Never, never get the flu shot." I was so happy to write home to Mom and Daddy that I was allergic to eggs. Mom felt guilty and sorry for all the "torture" she had inflicted upon me.

As the clock was ticking for my departure, I felt I was inflicting pain on my entire family due to the decision I had made. I sensed the change in the dynamics of our family life. There was little spontaneity and sharing at the supper table. My mother tried her best to buoy the conversations, but with little success. I became a silent observer. I ate very little, even passing up apple pie a-la-mode. The night before I left home, I did not show up for the evening meal, and no one urged me to come and eat. That last supper with the vacant chair had to evoke strong emotions within Mom, Daddy and my siblings, as I remained upstairs in my room, drowning in my thoughts. Later, Daddy came upstairs and offered his fatherly advice: "Be obedient. Do what you are told to do; follow the rules. If for whatever reason, you feel you have made the wrong choice, our doors are always open to you."

August 28, 1946, finally arrived. I arose at three in the morning and clad myself in black and white. While putting on my stockings, Margaret questioned, "Do you really know what you are doing?"

I gave no reply. The truth of the matter was that I really did not know since I had yet to experience what was yet to come. Betty and Theresa stood like forlorn orphan girls as they said goodbye at the top of the stairway. Then Betty said, "I'm going to miss your bedtime stories," as she held back the tears. Kathleen, age nine, and Charles, seven, were too young to grasp the magnitude of my decision as they sadly waved goodbye still dressed in their pajamas.

I glanced at myself in the mirror and saw a new me. My family saw a different me. As I walked on the front porch, I noticed my cousin Raymond Donohue in the driver's seat of his car. I wondered where Daddy was. Wasn't he driving me to the train station?

Little did I realize that when Daddy came upstairs the night before, he was bidding me farewell. Years later, Mom told me he was so broken up over my leaving home that he did not want me to see his emotional response that morning. He felt he was giving me up for life, although the rules of the School Sisters of St. Francis were not as strict as the School Sisters of Notre Dame. Daddy had seven cousins in that order and was well aware of their rules regarding family visits. After I had become a sister and was home visiting my parents, Monsignor Fischer said to me, "If you had known how you broke your father's heart, you would never have left for the convent." Years later, my soft-hearted dad said to me, "I thought I was giving you up for life, but now, since the other children are married and have their own families, you are the only one I have left."

I looked at the clock. The train waits for no one. Mom and I went to the car, greeted Raymond and Sister Felicia who sat in the back seat, and without anytime to lose, we were on our way to Bonnots Mill. As we traveled down the winding roads at 3:30 a.m., darkness and silence prevailed. Silence was the only language that could be spoken and understood as we waited for the train.

Within ten minutes, the train curled around the bluff with its shrill whistle piercing the darkness. It was haunting to me and filled with mystery as Raymond flagged the train to stop. Sister Felicia bid adieu to Mom and Raymond and boarded the train. I thanked my cousin for being our chauffeur and then kissed Mom goodbye. She was "smiling on the outside and crying on the inside." What a courageous woman she was as her daughter, age 14, quickly boarded the train seeking her destiny in life.

As soon as I stepped into the coach, I burst into tears and held on to the seats as I walked down the aisle. I did not look out the window to wave a final goodbye to Mom. "He who puts his hands to the plow and looks back is not worthy of the Kin(g)dom of God" plagued my mind. I did not and could not look back.

Sister Felicia sensed the sadness of breaking away. She allowed me to be alone with my thoughts. Even the conductor felt sorry for me and tried to comfort me with his kind words. When I reflect on that day, tears still flow down my cheeks. It was one of the saddest days of my life.

After two and a half hours, the conductor announced our arrival in St. Louis. I was enamored by the majesty and beauty of Union Station, which was built by French immigrants. There was little time to savor the history and beauty as we proceeded to board the Abraham Lincoln bound for Chicago.

The porterman assisted us in getting on the train. This was a plush train with a dining car where meals were served on linen tablecloths with silverware. The black, male waiters dressed in black pants, white shirts and bow ties served the passengers. Under the circumstances, I really could not enjoy all that the train ride offered, although many years thereafter, I looked forward to taking the Abraham Lincoln when visiting my family.

By this time, the sun was out in full glory as we whizzed by many cornfields. Even through my tearful eyes, I noticed immediately the flat land in Illinois in contrast to the hills and bluffs of Missouri. As a farm girl, I could appreciate the rich, black soil of Illinois, but trees were conspicuous by their absence.

For the most part, I was non-conversant on this trip, so Sister Felicia prayed the rosary, read a book and prayed from a *Manual of Prayers* and the *Little Office of the Blessed Virgin Mary*. I prayed, but not from a book. I ate several chocolates from a box of candy my Aunt Barbara Stolz had given me and shared the assortment with Sister Felicia. That was the extent of my eating. I had no desire for food.

After six hours of traveling, stopping at stations along the way, I saw the tall buildings of Chicago on the skyline. Unfortunately at that time, I thought of this city as a place of gangsters. As the train snailed into the long, dark entrance, I envisioned a gangster hiding behind every pillar. Later in life when I attended Loyola University and the Berlitz School of Foreign Languages, I grew to love Chicago.

The conductor loudly proclaimed "Chicago, Chicago! All passengers off!" Everyone seemed to be in a hurry. Hundreds of people walked briskly into the station. I had been accustomed to a slower pace, but Sister and I picked up our tempo and moved with the crowd that also came from several other trains.

We now had to transfer to a train going to Milwaukee. The station was filled with people of color. I felt so insignificant as we ventured through this huge and beautiful architectural wonder. I never had such an experience before. We passed by a little shop that sold postcards. Sister Felicia bought a card and said, "We have to wait for the next train, so you may want to send a card to your family." I was happy she made that suggestion. When my dad died, we went through his trunk that held many important documents. To my surprise, this card was among them. I was deeply touched after all these years that Daddy treasured that little postcard. However, writing the card was another reminder that I was no longer at home. The tears began to flow no matter how hard I tried to suppress them. We boarded the Milwaukee Road as I wondered what I was yet to face and experience this day.

After a long and emotional day, we arrived in Milwaukee. We took a cab to 1501 South Layton Boulevard, which is not far from the train station. St. Joseph Convent is in the city, not near Lake Michigan as I had envisioned. My heart skipped a few beats as the cab stopped. There before me was a huge, imposing structure on an entire city block. The dirty, sooty convent was enclosed by a wrought-iron fence with bars on all the first-floor windows. I was horrified and thought I was entering a prison. Behind Sister Felicia's back, I hailed the cab, but the driver did not see me as he drove off. In retrospect, that was a blessing. Who knows what my life might have been. As I looked at the stern building, I said to myself, "Well, I'm here, so I may as well go inside and see what it's like."

The two of us walked up a flight of wide cement steps that led to the second floor. Sister rang the doorbell. The huge, wooden door opened and there stood a young sister from China, Sister Mary Agnes Jen. "Welcome to our home,"

St. Joseph Convent main entrance to second floor from 1890-1969

she greeted in Oriental fashion. I will never forget that moment. When I stepped over the threshold, it was like going from battle to victory, from darkness to light. A peace came over me that I had never felt before, or experienced to that degree again in my life. I knew that I had made the right decision in answering God's call.

St. Joseph Convent with the first floor entrance

Chapter IV
Life in the Convent

The interior of St. Joseph Convent was a striking contrast to the sooty exterior. Little did I realize at that time that this building constructed in 1890, reflected European architecture, since our foundresses had come from Germany in 1874. Consequently, the outside steps led to the main entrance on the second floor. On either side of the lobby were large art parlors with huge paintings copied from the masters by sister artists. The prison image immediately took flight as I witnessed not only the parlors, but the long corridors decked with incredible artistry.

I was happy that, in the 1960s the brick building was sandblasted, the bars and a portion of the wrought-iron fence were removed, which made the exterior compatible to the life inside. The outside steps to the second floor were eliminated and the entrance was transferred to the first floor.

My limited knowledge of convent life began expanding as I was escorted to the refectory, a new term to me, to eat supper. We walked down a large oak stairway to a room called St. Isidore where many young women aspiring to be sisters were seated at tables. My mother often said to me when I was seeking attention and becoming self-centered, "You aren't the only pebble on the beach." Now more than ever I realized the reality of this statement. I was one among many.

After riding the train all day, I should have been hungry, but the strangeness and newness of my environment did not stimulate my appetite. Instead of conversing at the meal, we listened to someone read from a book on spiritual matters. Feeding my soul did not nourish me when I was curious about those sitting around me. Where did they come from? Are they as bewildered as I am? My thoughts also tiptoed back to my family. This was my first meal away from home, and I already missed them.

When we finished eating, we proceeded upstairs to a room for recreation named St. Gabriel. I met several aspirants and began to feel I would have no trouble making friends. Each one I met said to me, "I love your accent. Where are you from?" Arlene from Iowa asked, "Where did you get that southern drawl? I love it." This astounded me.

I had not a clue that I had an accent or a southern drawl. As I engaged in conversation with them, I felt they were the ones with an accent.

When I went to confession for the first time at St. Joseph Convent, the chaplain, who was not like the priests I had had at home, asked me if I was a foreigner. He made me repeat my confession three times and told me to go to another priest because he couldn't understand me. That did it for me! I left the confessional without absolution. Did he think this foreigner had committed a crime, or what? I walked out in tears, wondering if I really had a vocation. Thank God, Sisters Juan Hubl and Viola Blissenbach, our directors, consoled and assisted me in keeping afloat.

After recreation, we had night prayer and then we were off to St. Sebastian dorm, which was in a wing on the first floor. There were rows of beds neatly made with white bedspreads. By each bed was a night stand and curtains that could be drawn to enclose the cell.

Dormitories were a way of life for School Sisters of St. Francis. Five hundred of us, including novices and professed sisters lived in this five-story building sprawled across a city block. Dormitories were also a place of silence. When we retired, we observed the practice called The Great Silence. By that time, most sisters were too tired to talk, so it really did not matter. I was certainly ready for my first dorm experience. All I remember before I fell into a deep sleep was praying, "Thank you, God. I made it this far."

Morning came too fast as someone proclaimed at 5:00, "Jesus lives," to which we responded "Eternal love," hardly audible because we were still half asleep. After several weeks, we learned the prayers that were prayed aloud in the dorm on rising, washing and dressing. I still remember the prayer that we recited when putting on our religious garb.

> As now I vest my body with my religious garb, thus do Thou O Lord, vest my soul with Thy grace, that I may walk the path of thy Commandments. O Mary, my Mistress and my Mother, I give myself entirely to thee. I consecrate to thee this day, my eyes, my ears, my mouth, my heart, my whole being without reserve. Wherefore, good Mother, as I am thy own, keep me, guard me, as thy property and possession.

> … JESUS, MEEK AND HUMBLE OF HEART, MAKE MY HEART LIKE UNTO THINE…

Everyone rose promptly and hurried to do the routine rituals of getting ready to begin a new day. I was not accustomed to the speed

St. Joseph Chapel

I sensed from the girls around me. They were from Chicago, I later learned, and Milwaukee. One thing I grasped quickly was to be on time for all activities; however, I had already learned that discipline from home. The only difference was that I had to allow more time to get from one place to the other because of the vastness of the building.

Shortly before 7:00 a.m., we marched into chapel for Mass where the novices and professed sisters had already assembled to pray the Little Office of the Blessed Virgin Mary. This was the greatest experience of all for me. St. Joseph Chapel, situated on the second floor without an outside entrance (that's why it is called a "chapel") is a worship space of incomparable beauty. I had never seen such a cathedral. The beautiful church in Frankenstein could not stand up to the majesty and beauty of this historical landmark of Milwaukee.

I later learned more about the chapel where I would be spending many hours in worship and prayer. Mother Alfons Schmid, co-foundress of our order, felt that "nothing is too perfect for the House of God," so she began making plans for this dream chapel. She commissioned Milwaukee church architects Peter Brust and Richard Phillipp to pursue this dream with her. Phillipp went to Europe to study famous cathedrals before this perfect example of Italian Romanesque Revival style appeared on the drawing board. Construction began in 1913 and was completed in 1917. The chapel, 200 feet long and 90 feet wide

Mosaic of the "Five Foolish Virgins and Five Wise"

at its greatest breadth, seats 500. The dome rises 70 feet above the sanctuary. You can understand why I was overwhelmed my first time in this chapel. That morning, when we gathered for Mass, the entire chapel was filled with sisters and young women in formation.

The altars, exquisitely carved of pure Italian Carrara marble are inlaid with multi-colored stones. The high altar displays the statues of St. Francis on the left, St. Joseph in the Center and St. Clare on the right. Why does St. Joseph occupy center stage when we are a Franciscan order? Our foundresses had great devotion to St. Joseph, who assisted them in coming and settling in America during numerous trials and many sorrows, such as the devastating fire that destroyed the first motherhouse. The chapel was consecrated on March 19, 1917, the feast of St. Joseph.

Other noteworthy features of the chapel are the masterfully executed mosaics created in Innsbruck, Austria. One hundred fifteen windows of art glass, imported from Innsbruck, illumined the chapel. This is the greatest collection of Austrian stained glass in the United States. The Stations of the Cross are one-of-a-kind, hand carved hard maple from St. Ulrich, Switzerland. The pews crafted in fumed oak with "pierced work," a Byzantine influence, were made in La Crosse, Wisconsin.

What is utterly amazing is that the chapel was built during World War I and most everything was imported and arrived safely from Europe during that time. A story is told of Mother Alfons receiving a Western Union telegram stating that one of the shipments was unsafe to send. Mother Alfons wired back, "Send it; we will pray."

As I knelt in chapel waiting for Mass to begin, I was mesmerized by the beauty surrounding me. The thought occurred to me that this is a place where all the prayers of the past unite with my prayers and all present here. I felt there was no better place to be than St. Joseph Convent.

My decision was even more confirmed when the bell rang for Mass and the 75 voiced choir, under the direction of Sister Clarissima Neumann, sang the Introit in Gregorian Chant. Those notes rose to the vaulted dome in a crescendo of thanksgiving in my heart. St. John Chrysostom's words rang true: "Nothing will so elevate the soul and keep it on a higher sphere freed from the earth and bodily ties; nothing will so fill it with love of heavenly wisdom and the contempt of mortal affairs as melodious chant and the music of divine hymns."

The School Sisters of St. Francis have a rich heritage in liturgical music, and it was apparent at every daily Mass. In 1879, John B. Singenberger, a great musician, editor of *Caecilia* magazine, and reformer of Church music in America, began teaching music in the community. He, in his strict and dynamic way, started the sisters on an apostolate of liturgical music.

Sister Cerubim Schaefer playing an original composition

In 1924, the motherhouse offered music studies when Sister Cherubim Schaefer, acclaimed liturgical musician and composer, opened St. Joseph Convent Conservatory of Music. Under her leadership, the conservatory provided training for the congregation's music teachers, choir directors, and liturgical musicians at the parishes staffed by the sisters. Consequently, the sisters who taught me at St. Mary's were well trained in teaching music. In third grade we already learned Gregorian Chant and sang at Mass.

After Mass, we went to the refectory for breakfast. We silently took our places, prayed aloud and listened to table reading as we shared in this family-style meal: toast, oatmeal, scrambled eggs, and radishes. As I passed the bowl of oatmeal to the girl next to me, she quietly said, "Who ever heard of radishes for breakfast?" I had never had radishes for breakfast either. Was this a German custom? I liked radishes and really didn't care when they were served. In fact, they were much better than eggs; however, I was able to tolerate a small portion of the scrambled eggs that morning. Three days later, that girl did not appear at table. Was it the radishes? I don't know.

Each aspirant had daily work after breakfast. I cleaned a stairway which was a simple task for me. With so many people assigned cleaning jobs, the entire building was spotless. Thereafter, when we scrubbed long terrazzo corridors, I felt it was more to keep us busy than to remove dirt. "Idleness is the devil's workshop," was a statement we heard often from Sister Viola. Normally, after daily work, we went to classes for the entire day, but at this point, our classes had not yet been determined.

Without delay, we soon were given a choice: teacher, nurse, musician, artist, housekeeper. Because I had had piano lessons before entering, I chose to study music. Almost immediately I was assigned to classes and private piano, organ and violin lessons taught by sisters who were well educated in their professions. Thus began a four-year training program before I would be received into the order as a novice.

I took my studies seriously and worked hard to excel in every class. One of my favorite classes was English taught by Sister Berenice Brau. It was she who taught her students to love Shakespeare. I began writing my own poems in iambic pentameter. On one of the sonnets I had written, Sister Berenice wrote, "Who knows? You may someday be a Shakespeare." Such a comment was not only encouraging, but motivated me to write more poetry.

Sister Berenice also had the ability to comfort the students who suffered from homesickness. I was one of them. Especially during autumn, I missed the intense colors of the Missouri hills and bluffs, something I took for granted until I left home. In addition to her keen mind, she had an understanding heart. "This, too, will pass," she said to me. "It's good to experience homesickness and get it over with. I remember how homesick I was," she said with such compassion. To the delight of all, she also had a subtle sense of humor and used her gift well in class. I learned years later that it was Sister Berenice who was instrumental in assisting some of the other young women to persevere in religious life.

The music department presented some memorable experiences for me. Sister Anna Huber, my violin teacher from Germany, had perfect pitch. Once, while I was having a lesson, the bells of St. Lawrence Church across the street were ringing, a fire truck came clanging down Greenfield Avenue, a police siren whizzed down Layton Boulevard, and I was playing a concerto in the key of G. This conglomeration of sounds, all in different pitches, gave Sister Anna a violent headache. She told me her "great gift is also a great curse."

Later, when I became a novice, I was placed in the soprano section next to Sister Anna on the risers in the choir loft. At my violin lesson one day, she said to me, "I wanted to put a sheet of paper under you this morning at Mass." Believe me, I did all in my power to sing on pitch so I would not give her a headache!

My most memorable lesson with Sister Anna was when I had learned to play Camille Saint-Saens' "The Swan" perfectly in tune and with great expression. She was so pleased with my performance that she removed her Amati (not original) from the case, handed her violin to me

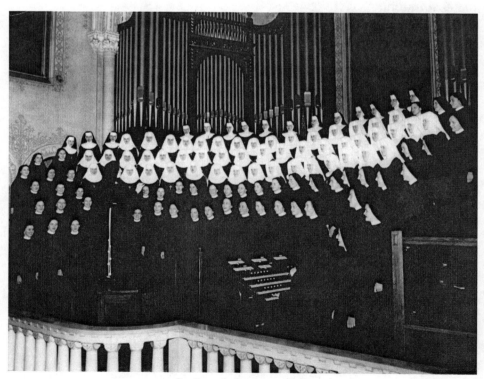

St. Joseph Convent Choir

and said, "Now I want you to hear yourself play this on my violin." I was stunned! No one ever dared touch her violin. That was the only time in my life I had the thrill of playing an Amati and hearing myself perform with passion this beautiful composition. Needless to say, to this day when I hear "The Swan," I think of this special time with Sister Anna.

I was in a piano performance class and played J. S. Bach, "Invention No. 13 in A minor," as Sisters Xavaria Friedrich, Director of the Music Department, Seraphim Stoecker and Benedicta Fritz, my teacher, critiqued my playing. After I had finished playing, Sister Xavaria, who sat in the back of the room looking through binoculars said, "You have just murdered Bach." I thought I had done a terrific job—no mistakes and lots of feeling. That was the problem—too much feeling! "You don't play Bach like Robert Schumann," she said.

After this class, we went to chapel for weekly confession. Since confession was such a drag for me, I was always looking for something to confess. I said to the priest, "I just murdered Bach." "Really! Tell me more," he said, as he tried to subdue his laughter. To my delight, he gave me absolution.

Frequent confession was not the only custom at this period of history in the church and religious communities. There were many

Postulants in chapel

36

devotional practices: Forty Hours' Devotion, holy hours in our Perpetual Adoration Chapel, processions on the 25th of each month in honor of the Infant of Prague for vocations, novenas to St. Joseph, the Sacred Heart, etc. Consequently, in the aspirancy and postulancy, I spent many hours on my knees.

Meditation was also an integral part of our lives, especially as a postulant, which was the year we pursued our professional studies at Alverno College. It was much easier to pray from the *Manual of Prayers* that we were given. Meditation is the practice of being still. To take hold of our minds and calm our thoughts, we must also be aware of our feelings and perceptions. As the Zen masters stress, "To take hold of your mind, you must practice mindfulness of the mind." This was difficult in a community devoted primarily to "doing" rather than "being."

To assist us in the discipline of meditating, the candidates and sisters were given three volumes entitled: *Growth in the Knowledge of Our Lord, Meditations for Every Day* by Abbe DeBrandt, translated from the French by Mother Mary Fidelis. Our own printing department called the Seraphic Press printed these volumes as well as other publications for the community. Thus, the importance of developing us spiritually was manifested in many ways.

However, academics were equally as important. The very title, School Sisters of St. Francis, indicates our mission: "Go forth and teach," as the Gospel message proclaims. From the founding of the order, the teaching of youth was the chief apostolate achieved through vigorous sacrifices and even privations at that time.

I felt privileged to be a part of this community that had already established a national reputation in the field of education. I often reflected on my options. Had I remained in Frankenstein, would I have had the opportunities and exposure I am now experiencing? Even though I would have gone to college, as did all my siblings, how would my life have been different? Would I have persevered in my calling to be a sister?

I entered the School Sisters of St. Francis, an international community, during the Renaissance of the order in the late 40s and 50s. Mother Corona Wirfs was the Superior General whose mind was as expansive as the horizon. Our membership was over 4,500. We were recognized as a great teaching order and achieved worldwide recognition for our music.

Because of our acclaim in music, Fernando Germani, the Vatican organist, performed in our chapel. When he heard our orchestra, he said, "I wish I could put all of you on a plane and have you play for Pope Pius XII, who loves music." Every Sunday afternoon, Mr. Germani played a one-hour Bach concert for Pope Pius XII. I played second violin in the orchestra and delighted in hearing about the Pope's parakeet that perched on his shoulder when shaving in the morning.

Sister Theophane Hytrek,
organist and composer

Marcel Dupré from France, considered the world's greatest organist at that time, also performed in the chapel. When he heard Sister Theophane Hytrek play the organ, he said, "She is greater than I."

Leonard Pennario, renowned American classical pianist and composer, performed in St. Joseph Hall. I can still see the red socks he wore as he sat on the piano bench. It was such a contrast to his dark trousers. I thought it was funny. Was he trying to "knock the socks off our feet?"

Dr. Mario Salvador, St. Louis Cathedral organist, consulted Sister Theophane regarding a composition he was writing and gave a concert. Other performers, liturgical musicians and composers such as Alexander Peloquin, Joseph Gelineau, and Jean Langlais, contributed to the rich culture and heritage of the School Sisters of St. Francis.

Playing in the orchestra under the direction of Sister Marcina Schlenz, a dynamic conductor, was one of the exhilarating experiences of my life. I will never forget the feeling of performing Dvorak's "New World Symphony," Beethoven's "Fifth Symphony," and Brahms "Symphony in E Minor." Producing harmony together in an orchestra is an experience I could never have gained from a book or any other source. We gave public concerts to the religious and clergy of the archdiocese, the Knights of Columbus, and other organizations. On special feast days, the orchestra entertained the sisters and women in formation.

Orchestra of the School Sisters of St. Francis

Pat O'Brien, the movie star, gave a talk in St. Joseph Hall; however, I cannot recall anything he said, even though he has more than 100 screen credits. He played Irish cops and priests primarily. What I do remember was his delightful and engaging personality.

Social activist, Dorothy Day, was a guest speaker who spoke about the Catholic Worker Movement in 1938; she also returned to the Motherhouse about ten years later when I was privileged to hear her. I soon learned that our community was heavily invested in justice and peace and concern for the poor.

As an aspirant and postulant, I was striving to be a "poor Franciscan," a phrase our directors often emphasized. But periodically I asked myself, "What is poverty?" As Americans, we tend to think of poverty in terms of money—economic deprivation. Was I really poor? Where could I have gone; what could I have done to have received the discipline, education, cultural, spiritual, mental, physical development that I attained in formation as a School Sisters of St. Francis? I considered myself rich; I was filled with Franciscan joy.

Even though I am forever grateful for all that I received from the community, it was apparent during these formative years that the topic of sex was never discussed, not even "the birds and the bees." Those were the years when feelings and passions could have run amuck were it not for the controlled environment and discipline of convent life. I'm grateful that my mother prepared me for the basics in life like menstruation, sexual intercourse, pregnancy. Her advice to her daughters was "make yourself precious"—something I did not fully appreciate and even understand until later in dealing with relationships with men. When my sisters and I deviated somewhat from the path of righteousness, Mom repeatedly said to us in her drawn out southern style, "It's a sin and a shame the way you girls act." In her advanced years, we told her that this was the epitaph we were inscribing on her tombstone. We still quote her today even though she is no longer in our midst.

In community life, the development of wholesome, human sexuality was not a part of our spiritual, physical, and emotional growth. If anything, there was denial that we were sexual beings. The rational was stressed to the exclusion of the biological. Is it any wonder when the rules were relaxed in the mid 60's many young women left community life and married, although some chose to remain single. What is so sad is that our human sexuality was repressed and not recognized as a precious, God-given gift to each of us.

That was then. Now, women in formation have workshops, conferences, discussions on topics related to sexuality. In the common novitiate, where several orders, including our own, have established a center in St. Louis for women, there are also periodic sessions with men of religious communities. Sexuality is dealt with in a much broader, human, wholesome, life-giving way.

Family picture taken at a home visit when I was an aspirant, 1948
Back: Betty, Mom, Barbaralie, Daddy
Front: Theresa, Charles, Kathleen, Margaret

Chapter V
Becoming a Novice

On the morning of June 13, 1950, in St. Joseph Convent Chapel, Milwaukee, I took the first step in becoming a "spouse of Christ," which meant at that time I was marrying Christ.

As I walked up the aisle in a bridal veil, I realized this was a profound and sacred moment in my life. Archbishop Moses Elias Kiley asked, "Do you for the love of God still ask for the habit in this community of the School Sisters of St. Francis?"

Seventy-four other postulants and I answered in one accord, "We humbly ask for it." During the next hour, the other postulants and I laid aside our last temporal adornment, as Shakespeare said "woman's crowning glory." As we stepped up to the altar railing, the archbishop cut a lock of hair saying:

> May the Lord take from your heart the pomp of the world which you renounced when you received Baptism. Amen.

The archbishop then gave the folded habit and scapular to each of us saying:

> May the Lord invest you with the vestment of salvation and may He clothe you with the garment of his justice. Take the sweet yoke of the Lord upon you that you may find rest to your soul.

We then processed out of chapel into St. Joseph Hall to be clothed in the habit and scapular.

During this time, Sister Theophane gave an organ concert and the choir sang several polyphonic selections in the chapel filled with our parents and many priests in the sanctuary. I was saddened when I received word that Father Rost, who was so much a part of my journey, was very ill with leukemia and was unable to be at my reception.

Sister Sponsaria (Angela) Schmitz, my cousin, assisted in helping me dress in the habit. She first cut off my curls so as to make it easier to put on all the white pieces around my neck, forehead and face. I won't forget the initial feeling of tightness and discomfort wondering if I would ever be able to eat and swallow again. I also wondered how I looked in all this head gear. There were no mirrors in the convent at that time.

Postulants in bridal veils about to become novices

After we were clad in the habit and wearing our black postulant veil, we processed up the aisle for the ceremony to continue. I spotted my mother and dad in tears in the middle of chapel next to the middle aisle as they glanced at me. The drama and pageantry of becoming a sister were like none other and brought tears to many who witnessed this sacred formality.

As we knelt at the communion railing, Archbishop Kiley with the assistance of a sister behind each candidate, removed the black veil and placed the white veil of a novice on our heads saying:

> Receive, O daughter this covering of the head as a sign of purity and chastity; may it be to you the beginning of all perfection. In the name of the Father, and of the Son and of the Holy Ghost. Amen.

We then were given the cincture with five knots representing the five wounds of Christ. The cincture is a distinct Franciscan symbol representing the stigmata of our Seraphic Father, St. Francis.

> May the Lord gird you with the cincture of this Order according to the invocation of his most holy name and that of our holy Father Francis, so that you can be mindful of the cords and Passion of our Lord, Jesus Christ and eagerly desire works of penance and charity. Amen.

Giving the Rule Book, the archbishop said:

> Receive this rule. Observe it faithfully, and God will give you eternal life. Amen.

Presenting the crucifix that we were to wear, he said:

> Receive, O daughter, this sign of the holy cross; may it be for you a source of consolation, a protection and guard against the cruel attacks of the enemy, through Christ our Lord. Amen.

Then we were each given a lighted candle:

> Receive the light of Christ as a sign of your immortality that being dead to the world you may live for God. Amen.

Placing a crown of flowers on the head, he said:

> Receive the crown of virginal excellence, so that as you are crowned by this hand of earth you may merit to be crowned by Christ with glory

and honor in heaven. Amen.

And then the moment came that kept most of us in suspense. Each of us held a folded slip of paper in our hands bearing the new name we were to be given as a sister. Previously, we were permitted to suggest three names, but there was no assurance that we would receive any of the names. Many postulants took a combination of their parents' names, as Joseph Clare. I couldn't think of any combination with my parents, Gertrude and August, so requested to have my baptismal name since no one else in the order had that name. Acquiring a new name reflected biblical times when an individual underwent conversion and was given a new mission. Thus Saul became Paul; Abram became Abraham.

The sister before me received the name Mary Hope. I thought for sure I would be Faith or Charity. The master of ceremonies, Father John Grow, removed the slip of paper from my fingers and handed it to the archbishop.

Your name in religion will be Sister Mary Avellino. Strive to bear it in a worthy manner.

I made a face showing my dislike of the name, as Father Grow handed the slip of paper back to me with a big grin. I later found out

Barbaralie's reception into the School Sisters of St. Francis, June 13, 1950

44

from Sister Thomasine Nels, who was Mother Corona's secretary, that she chose the name for me because it's musical and the configuration is beautiful.

The name served me well in my second teaching assignment in Warrenville, Illinois, where there were many Italians. They loved the name and said it in Italian style—Ave-llino. Every Friday evening, we sisters received Italian pastries, pastas, and pizzas because the people thought I was Italian. After months of Italian indulgences, one of the sisters said, "Avellino, tell them you're not Italian!"

I grew to love the name after Saint Andrew Avellino, whose feast day was November 10th. Interestingly enough, most of the School Sisters of St. Francis still called me Barbaralie. Only the people I served on mission, who knew me by no other name, called me Avellino.

When I was at the motherhouse during the summer for retreat in the mid 60s, I met Sister Francis Borgia Rothluebber, our president, in the corridor. I asked her if I may go back to my baptismal name and gave her the reason. Before she could respond, Sister Joanne Wolsfelt, my classmate, came down the corridor and said, "Hi, Barbaralie! It's so good to see you!" Sister Francis Borgia could tell this was not staged. She said, "I can't make that decision alone. Write a letter to me and I will consult the Council." Within two weeks the entire order received a letter stating that they were permitted to return to their baptismal names if they chose to do so.

But I digressed. After the elaborate ceremony and Mass were over, we went to the refectory for lunch, and our parents were escorted to the visitors' department for a simple meal. I could hardly wait to see Mom and Daddy since we had not seen each other in a year. I looked for them in the convent garden and spotted my mother in her big, beautiful hat, so characteristic of her. We hugged each other, and I could tell she delighted in embracing her Barbaralie, who was now Sister Avellino. She looked at me in the habit and said, "You are beautiful."

Daddy had wandered off in the garden with his own thoughts and emotions. I did not see him anywhere, and chose not to look for him, but just let him be. I knew the ceremony was emotional and difficult for him. After about an hour, he joined Mom and me. The tears were still apparent as he embraced me. He tried to make light of the moment by saying, "Your mom and I chose the names of saints at your baptism. Now you become a nun and get the name of a town in Italy." I replied, "Because there are so many of us, I'm just glad I didn't get a number."

Mom, in her beautiful singing voice, broke out in song:

Down in the valley where the lilies first bloomed,
There lived a little girl as sweet as a rose,
Dear Avellino, sweet Avellino,
My love for you will never, never die.

How great it was to hear Mom's voice again, which brought back so many childhood memories.

After a wonderful afternoon, catching up on all the family who could not be present for my reception, our time together had come to an end. Because of the large group of 75 being received, only parents were invited. The chapel and the balcony were filled to capacity.

It was hard to say goodbye to Mom and Daddy. The tears flowed gently down our faces. I watched them as they walked down the steps to the street until I could see them no more. I closed my eyes for a brief time and felt the essence of their love within me, inseparable from who I am. After all the excitement of the day, I now listened to the silence around me. I was at peace.

Each day of my novitiate, I lived the meaning of my reception day. During the first year of the novitiate, I spent a great part of the day in prayer, and in the study of Holy Scripture, the vows, the Rule, and the Constitutions of the congregation. A few hours of each day were devoted to manual work.

I was assigned to help Sister Johanna Endres in the sacristy along with two other novices. It was a privilege cleaning and dusting in the House of God. Other novices worked in the laundry, the bakery, the printing department, the priests' quarters and the kitchen.

True to the Franciscan teaching that work is grace, we earnestly pursued the science of sanctity. We soon learned that it is not what we do that leads to sanctity, but how we do it and with what motive. Often we prayed the rosary aloud while doing menial tasks.

Sister Johanna had me help her make bouquets for the altars. I loved working with flowers and took great pains making beautiful floral arrangements. When I made my first bouquet, I proudly placed it on the altar of the Blessed Mother. Sister Johanna later had me remove the bouquet and bring it back into the sacristy. She said, "Sister, I want to teach you how to improve on this bouquet." I was not offended. I was eager to learn from someone who had studied Japanese floral arrangements. In addition to that, she was an artist by profession and specialized in charcoal portraits and watercolor.

I profited by her patience and teaching when I was sent to St. Irene Parish in Warrenville, Illinois, as a teacher, organist and sacristan. The parishioners and pastor often complimented me on the beautiful bouquets. This seemed to have motivated people to keep bringing flowers to the church, sometimes more than I could handle. On big feast days, the other sisters assisted in adorning the altars with flowers.

In addition to sacristy work as a novice, I still practiced organ, piano and violin, went to my weekly music lessons and played in the orchestra. It was important for musicians to maintain their skills, whereas the teachers and nurses observed the canonical mandate of a year devoted to prayer and manual labor.

The novices who passed the audition sang in the chapel choir. We practiced daily for one hour. On several occasions, we did recordings for the Jesuit Sacred Heart Program aired from St. Louis. After we had eaten breakfast, we literally stood on the choir for one entire day doing recordings. Our training in singing was equal to private voice lessons.

As novices, we had a Holy Hour in our Perpetual Adoration Chapel from 2:00 a.m. to 3:00 a.m. The combination of first and second-year novices numbered approximately 150. Therefore, we did not get a turn that often since only two novices were appointed for the hour. I always looked forward to this time before the Blessed Sacrament even though I was deprived of sleep. I liked the quiet of the early morning and found it to be a special time to pray for my loved ones at home as well as the congregation.

Sister Archelaus Markowski

In accordance with the Rule, we assembled for recreation twice each day, between the hours of prayer and work. Recreational activities varied. Sometimes we pinned up our skirts and played basketball and volleyball. It's amazing how adept we became in those long skirts! Often we made up skits and composed words and music for special events, or an appreciation for our wonderful novice director, Sister Archelaus Markowski, who held that position for 26 years. She enjoyed our

Novices folk dancing for recreation

creativity that provided wonderful entertainment.

One thing we learned early in religious life is that "particular friendships" were outlawed. When I saw individuals being sent home for not observing this rule, I knew this was a serious violation. Consequently, I managed at work, in class, at recreation to weave in and out of relationships so as not to be accused of a particular friendship. Am I proud of this achievement? No, I regret that I never really got to know the members of my class, nor did they get to know me. This was certainly a violation of my extroverted personality and in no way did it enhance my spirituality. The wonderful thing is that I was sent on mission in my early years and acquired deep and abiding friendships with the sisters with whom I lived and worked, as well as with many parishioners. We had no time and energy to dwell on particular friendships when we were focused on our ministries.

It was during the novitiate that we had a sewing class to learn how to make our habits. Sister Angelyn (Mary) Dingman, assistant novice director, had the patience of a saint in teaching and assisting us. Fortunately, I had learned to sew in 4-H Club at home, but I witnessed other novices in tears as they struggled to make our pleated and tailored habit. During sewing class, I was scheduled for a piano lesson, so I was not a part of this learning experience. Sister Angelyn periodically checked to see how I was progressing.

We were each given a bolt of material. When I saw all this yardage, I thought it was enough for two habits, so I cut the material in half. I worked diligently to complete this enormous task and proudly walked up to Sister Archelaus holding both habits in my hands to show her my finished work. She looked at me in utter astonishment. "How did you end up with two habits?" she asked. "I had so much material that I cut it in half," I replied. With a twinkle in her eye, she said, "That was to be for one habit whether you are thin or obese. Our Rule, approved by Rome, states 3-1/2 English yards." Without thinking, I blurted out, "That is a stupid rule." I soon learned to think before speaking. After she checked my sewing, Sister said, "Well, go ahead and wear the habits."

In my second year as a novice, I continued studies and followed an abbreviated program at Alverno College that was owned and operated by our congregation. Initially, the college not only educated our sisters, but other women religious from around the country. Today, Alverno is a women's college of national and international acclaim for its teaching and learning based on its eight-abilities curriculum. Fortunately, I have been on the Board of Trustees since 2002.

I'm sure many of you are asking, "What is reception into the School Sisters of St. Francis like today?" First of all, since we may no longer choose to wear a habit, much of the drama as I experienced is history. Secondly, we no longer have large numbers of women entering and being received in the order. That is also history. It is not my purpose in this autobiography to give a social analysis as to why the big change in our society, culture, and the Catholic church.

Alverno College

The ceremony today is equally as beautiful, profound, and meaningful. The United States Provincial asks the affiliate:

What do you ask of us?

To which she replies:

Drawn by God's inspiration and the love of Francis of Assisi, I have come here to learn your way of life. I ask you to lead me to follow

49

Christ and to live in poverty, obedience, and chastity. Show me how to persevere in prayer and penance and to live out the Gospel every day of my life. Teach me your rule, and together with me, continue to learn how to love and serve those with whom I share this earth, as Christ commanded.

The provincial then expresses acceptance of the candidate, followed by a blessing and presentation of symbols: the Tau Cross, our community emblem since we removed the veil; *Response in Faith: Rule of Life*; a lighted candle, and the title "Sister" along with her baptismal name. The liturgy allows for the creative input of the candidate herself. She has something to say about the music, hymns, and readings and who is the celebrant and homilist.

The symbolism of the Tau cross, official emblem of the School Sisters of St. Francis, relates themes from pagan and biblical times and days of St. Francis. Because the Tau cross is the official emblem of the School Sisters of St. Francis and is a way of identifying us, allow me to explain its significance. The word "Tau" comes from the 19th letter of the Greek alphabet. In early civilization, the joined vertical/horizontal lines of the Tau cross were symbolic of human relationships supported  by a vertical relationship to the gods. St. Francis of Assisi in 13th century Italy was so awed with the significance of the Tau cross that he adopted this as the official symbol of his order. A reading from Ezekiel particularly moved him. The prophet spoke of "God's faithful ones being marked with the Tau on their foreheads." Francis exclaimed, "This shall be the mark of the Friars Minor, the faithful ones of the Lord." That is what the Tau means to the School Sisters of St. Francis. Whether the Tau cross is on a pin, a pendant, or a ring, it is a mark of one signed by the Lord, of one consecrated, commissioned, committed.

Now that I had completed two years of novitiate, I was ready to begin my profession retreat. The final month of preparation for an event so sublime and meaningful, which seemed at one time so far away, had come at last.

Chapter VI
Professing the Vows of Poverty, Chastity and Obedience

On June 21, 1952, I stood in the vestibule of chapel along with 75 other novices anxiously waiting for the music to begin. As the choir sang "Jesu Corona Virginem," we processed up the aisle on our Profession Day. The English version of this hymn is as follows and sets the stage for what was about to happen.

Jesu, the Virgin's crown, do Thou accept us as in prayer we bow;
Born of that Virgin, whom alone the Mother and the Maid we own.

Amongst the lilies Thou dost feed, by Virgin choirs accompanied—
With glory decked, the spotless brides whose bridal gifts Thy love provides.

They, wheresoe'er Thy footsteps lead with hymns and praises still attend;
In blessed troops they follow Thee, with dance, and song, and melody.

This hymn, filled with memories is still sung on jubilees and other occasions in the community.

As we lined up in front of chapel, the celebrant asked: "Venerable daughters in Christ! What do you ask?" We novices answered:

We ask to be admitted to the Profession of the School Sisters of St. Francis in this community, that by keeping our holy rule we may practice penance and better serve God.

Mother Corona Wirfs

Then kneeling before Mother Corona Wirfs, our Superior General, we publicly made our profession.

In the Name of the Father, and of the Son, and of the Holy Spirit. Amen.

I, Sister Mary Avellino Stiefermann, O.S.F., make the vows of poverty, chastity, and obedience in the Congregation of the Sisters of the Third Order of Penance of our Seraphic Father St. Francis and promise to God Almighty, before the Blessed and Immaculate Virgin Mary, before our Father St. Francis, before all the Saints of heaven, and into the hands of our Mother Mary Corona, O.S.F., that for one year, I will observe the Rule of the Sisters of the Third Order of Penance of our Seraphic Father St. Francis, and the Constitutions approved for our Congregation. May God with His Divine Grace, help me to do so.

Dated and signed by two witnesses, Mother Corona and Sister Avellino.

We then proceeded to the communion railing, and with the assistance of a professed sister, the white veil that we had worn as a novice was replaced with a black veil as the celebrant said:

Receive, O Brides of Christ, this sacred veil, by which you may be known to have forsaken the world and to have given truly and humbly with your whole heart and affection, yourselves forever as spouses to Christ Jesus, who will defend you from all evil and conduct you to life eternal. Amen.

The celebrant gave each of us a large black rosary to be worn on our left side with the words:

Receive the crown of the Blessed Virgin Mary; and so praise her by speech and deed that you always show yourselves worthy daughters of the Mother of God. Amen.

Placing a ring on our finger, he said:

I espouse you to Jesus Christ, who will keep you unharmed.

Giving a lighted candle to each sister, he said:

Receive this light into your hands that by this token you may learn to flee the works of darkness and through this new manner of living to strive after the deeds of light. Amen.

On Reception Day, a crown of flowers was placed on our heads. On Profession Day, a crown of thorns was placed on our head as the celebrant said:

Receive the emblem of that crown which your Savior wore on the Way of the Cross; suffer constantly with Christ in this life in order that you may have glory with Him in eternity. Amen.

Then came the most dramatic moment of all. As newly professed sisters, we prostrated ourselves and were covered with a pall as the choir sang:

You are dead and your life with Christ is hidden in God.

I remember exactly where I was lying in front of the altar of the Blessed Mother. This was a tearful part of the ceremony, not only for me, but for Mom and Daddy, and all other parents. To this day, when I walk on the spot where I was lying, I recall the words that were sung. When the pall was removed, the celebrant turned to us and sang:

Arise you, who sleep, arise from the dead and Christ will give you life.

I was happy to "rise from the dead" and begin my life as a professed sister.

Each year, for two consecutive years, I renewed vows; then I took vows for three years. After these six years, I took vows for life. My mother said to me on Perpetual Vow Day, "When I married your dad, I took him for 'better or for worse, for richer or for poorer, in sickness and in health, till death do us part.' I had only one chance at it; you've had six attempts before you made a life commitment." Was she advocating that the laws of marriage change? I don't know.

Sister Avellino (Barbaralie)
Perpetual Vows, 1958

Also, on this same day when I met my parents in the garden after the liturgy and lunch, Daddy said to me, "You may now become a sister." By this time he knew I was well on my journey and there was no turning back.

My sister Margaret and brother-in-law, Mike Powers, also attended my final profession. After they had returned to their home in Chicago, I received a letter from Mike.

June 22, 1958

Dear Sister Avellino,

It was good to be with you yesterday on such an especial occasion.
By way of afterthought, it has occurred to me that the mood of what
I witnessed is still strong upon me. Oh, the Irish mind for the love of
mood and mystery! And since the spoken word can sometimes be a
feeble instrument I merely want you to know now that if I live to be
a hundred I would never have the courage to do what your dedication
calls for.

I have always preferred to think that if the Good God lives anywhere,
he lives on a mountain crest, by the shores of some hidden lake, or in
the depths of the quiet sea. Now I'll have to add the Convent on Layton
Boulevard to my list.

Take care of yourself. We lesser humans need the knowledge that
somewhere there is someone who is not too involved with a 'world that
is too much with us.'

Love,
Mike

When I taught English at
Chaparral College, a career college
in Tucson, Arizona, the students
eventually discovered that I was
a sister, which prompted many
questions. During the course of the
discussion, I told them that I had taken
vows for life. I will never forget the
reaction of the entire class. They all
gasped aloud and spontaneously said
"for life?"

The response surprised me at the time, but after reflecting on the
outburst, I realized these students had rarely experienced permanency.
Many came from broken homes and had moved several times. A number
of the students had switched their majors and had attended different
colleges. Many of their parents had experienced several job and career
changes. The major permanency these students had experienced was
constant change. Permanent commitment seemed an impossibility to
them. Is it any wonder that the institution of marriage has significantly

changed?" Would it not be in the best interest of religious communities to consider temporary as well as permanent membership? There are a few communities that do renew vows each year. Do the three traditional vows have meaning to young adults today?

Stiefermann Family, late 1950s
Back: Theresa, Charles, Kathleen, Betty
Front: Sister Avellino, Daddy, Mom, Margaret

I took the vows of poverty, chastity, and obedience before the Second Vatican Council (1962-1965). Thus, I have lived the vows in two historical periods. In view of that experience, I want to reflect on the three traditional vows, looking at their original intent, and re-examine them in the context of the 21st century.

POVERTY

When I entered the community, the vow of poverty could have been perceived as a vow of dependency. I, personally, found it difficult to ask the superior for a tube of toothpaste, a pair of shoes, or five dollars. After we were permitted to drive, I had to ask for the use of the car. This changed after the Second Vatican Council, when we became responsible for budgeting and spending money.

Dependency was not the original intent of the vow of poverty. It was intended to take our minds and hearts away from the desire for wealth and worldly goods. Practically speaking, it became a vow of sharing, of being directly responsible for holding all things in common. We were invested in a group in which we shared ideals and possessions. Thus, our very language changed from "my" to "our," because we held all things in common.

As a Franciscan, the vow of poverty emphasizes our commitment to live simply without a surplus of worldly goods. Unfortunately, many bishops and Catholic school superintendents considered the vow of poverty as a basis of payment for service. In the past, salaries were extremely low, and in some parishes the sisters were not paid. Also, sisters were not covered under health insurance. Consequently, in the 60s and 70s, it was difficult for women religious leaders to negotiate with bishops and superintendents for adequate compensation and health insurance for services. This was a major shift, particularly in the field of education in parochial schools.

Having a budget and money to spend does not mean there are no limitations. We are conscious of satisfying "needs" more than "wants." We are a family; consequently, all the members are responsible and accountable toward one another.

So what might a vow in the 21st century look like? A person today might embrace "a vow of sharing" either with other community members, or even the world at large. Another possibility would be a "vow to live simply," especially relevant in a world crammed with commodities. Or, in

*Associates planting an organic garden
at St. Joseph Center*

an age where much emphasis is placed on climate change, individuals might consider a "vow to live ecologically," as some of our Associates are doing. (These are lay women and men who identify with the School Sisters of St. Francis values and mission).

One need not be a religious or celibate in taking vows of this nature. It's encouraging to witness the number of people who subscribe to these values.

CHASTITY

This vow is often misunderstood by many. Chastity is a virtue that requires someone to be faithful to his or her state of life or partner. Thus, a married person is considered chaste as long as he/she is faithful to his/her spouse.

In religious life, the vow of chastity entails the celibate lifestyle, or one might say a vow of celibacy. This means the religious lives without an exclusive or sexual love relationship with another human being. Simply stated, celibacy means the person is not married; however, the celibate would be unchaste if he/she had an affair with an individual.

What was the assumption surrounding the vow of chastity? It was thought that a primary love relationship such as marriage would distract from the love of God and neighbor. However, today many theologians think differently about this idea. I am in agreement with them. I think that an intimate human relationship could well enhance a person's love of God and others through one's ministries, one's community members, or the world at large. So what might this vow look like in the 21st century?

I recently met someone in a committed relationship who chose a vow of "fidelity in a loving relationship." This could be a vow for someone who is not in a committed relationship. Basically, this is a vow of faithfulness to God, whether as a celibate or a person in an already vowed relationship.

Sharing with people in need and rejecting the intolerances and divisions of races, ethnicity, class, gender and sexual orientation could be a "vow of solidarity," or a "vow to live compassionately." In a culture saturated with violence, "a vow to live nonviolently" could be a commitment embraced by both celibates and persons in vowed relationships.

I am not proposing something new. People are presently committing themselves to these vows. Already ten years ago, I heard discussions on the vows beyond the traditional meaning. In the case of chastity, would not these evolving vows take the emphasis off sexuality and direct it to a more expansive meaning of loving human relationships?

OBEDIENCE

It is important to consider the origins of this vow. In a world where royalty ruled, the vow of obedience was instituted. This was a time when bishops, abbots, abbesses were more educated than their subordinates and were assumed to know more about the needs of the larger world. Consequently, subjects were to obey them, especially in matters of ministry. It reflected a military model. Before Vatican II, I, as well as other sisters, were assigned to a specific parish or place to minister. This entailed working with other sisters who were also assigned to this place and living in a convent with them. Vatican II ushered in major changes. Sisters were allowed to choose both their ministries and living arrangements. In 1971, I chose to teach at St. Francis High School in Wheaton, Illinois. I chose to live with the Wheaton Franciscans who were in close proximity to the school. I had the use of a car (owned by the community). I welcomed having to go through interviews, rather than being assigned by Mother Superior. For some sisters, these changes were traumatic. Thus, the military model is history for sisters, which includes such titles as Mother General, superiors, "inferiors." Now we are encouraged to consult with leadership in a discernment process in making important decisions, such as a change in ministry. In the School Sisters of St. Francis and other communities, we are assumed to be adults in making decisions.

Obviously, the historic military-style interpretations of this vow are not compatible with the 21st century. Then what is the essence of the vow of obedience? Basically, one must be enabled to follow the Gospel call by figuring out how to live the example set by Jesus. As School Sisters of St. Francis, an international community,

> Our mission is to live the Good News of Jesus and witness to the presence of God as we enter into the lives and needs of people around the world, especially the poor. We are to be a source of new life, new meaning and new hope.

I, as well as others considering a form of committed life today, are well educated and highly informed about world issues. In my religious community, only college graduates and older women are accepted as viable candidates. We seek to have strong developed consciences and values.

I am not an isolated human being. I sometimes need the guidance and wisdom of other community members, but not for orders from above. This is where there is conflict today between Rome and the sisters in the United States. It is a conflict between pre- and post Vatican II theology. We, as women religious, took Vatican II seriously and made the changes proposed. Now we are chastised for doing so. It took 20 years after Vatican II for Rome to approve *Response In Faith: Rule of Life*, the Constitutions of the School Sisters of St. Francis. The battle over semantics was enough to make our sister-theologians and writers lose their sanity!

So how might this vow be expressed in a way that reflects the new reality? "Fidelity to Gospel values," which implies the person has not only studied the Gospels, but has conducted an honest probing of his/her conscience in a way that reflects the new reality. To put it simply, it could be "fidelity to an informed conscience."

OTHER VOWS

Even though I have professed to live the vows of poverty, chastity and obedience, I am not limited to those. What are other values that have relevance in today's world that I could commit myself to if I chose to do so?

- o Sharing goods with those in need
- o Caring for those in need
- o Living a life dedicated to justice and peace
- o Caring for Mother Earth
- o Offering hospitality
- o Speaking truth to power (the "prophetic" role of religious life)

Any of these vows can be lived as individuals, but as a member of a community, I find power and strength in bonding with other like-minded people, whether lay or religious.

With the decline of traditional vocations, we must open our hearts and minds to new possibilities. The communities of tomorrow will be different than experienced today. This does not mean I am predicting the demise of the three traditional vows of poverty, chastity, and obedience, but it does mean we need to envision new communities comprised of men and women; religious and lay, young and old. These communities would include the diversity of race, ethnicity, creed and sexual orientation, all of whom could rally around a specific cause or need in society. Some may choose to live in community; others may not. The important focus is the ministry and the development of the spiritual lives of the people involved.

The communities of tomorrow must evolve organically from within the people gathered for a common cause, not from leaders of religious orders and Rome. To artificially contrive a new order based on the old monastic model is doomed for failure. We must be open to the

Spirit to breathe forth new life.

A new life is already evolving; the Spirit is moving in ways yet to be realized. Developing, experimenting, welcoming and celebrating new forms of committed life need to be encouraged and accepted. After Vatican II renewal, we, the School Sisters of St. Francis revised the vow formula that the novices in my class of 1952 had professed. Were we to take vows today, the following form would be used.

U.S. Provincial......... What do you ask of God and us?

Novices.................. With the help of God, we have studied your rule and lived among you as your sisters for the time of Novitiate. Sister (Provincial), we now ask to be allowed to dedicate ourselves to the mission of Christ by making profession in this religious community of School Sisters of St. Francis.

U.S. Provincial......... May your lives be a continuing response to Christ's mission in the world. I am ready to witness your profession of vows.

Witnesses .... We are ready to witness your profession of vows.

Novices.................. I proclaim my belief in God, Creator, Redeemer, Sanctifier. I will be poor so that I may be more free to give. I will belong to Christ in love in order to be more free to love. I will obey the Spirit speaking in community so that I may be more free to serve. I, _____, vow to God poverty, chastity, obedience according to the Rule and Constitutions of the School Sisters of St. Francis.

I wish to live this faith commitment in community among the people of God. I ask Sister (Provincial) to accept my profession in the name of the Church and of our Congregation. May God and the people of God help me to fulfill what I have vowed.

U.S. Provincial......... In the name of God's holy people and the School Sisters of St. Francis, I accept your vowed commitment. May God who has begun this good work in you bring it to loving fulfillment.

Signing of Vow Papers by Novices and Witnesses

Blessing of Rings ...... Bless, O God, these rings. May they be shining symbols of love and dedication to you. Bless those who wear them. Give them faith, peace, good will, and love. We ask this through Christ our Lord. Amen.

Community Response You are the voice of the living God, calling us all to live in your love; to be people of God once again!

Sign of Peace

What were my thoughts and feelings after having taken the vows of poverty, chastity, and obedience for life? First of all, I had plenty of time to experience religious life before making this serious commitment. Secondly, if I had not been happy, I would have chosen to leave before final vows. I felt reasonably sure that I would persevere as a sister. What had not been tested to any great degree as yet was actually living those vows once I went on mission and left the safe, sheltered environment of the motherhouse.

The vows were put to the test early on, especially obedience and at times the vow of poverty. I was really tried in the fire during and after Vatican II renewal with the vow of chastity. I attended summer school at Loyola University in Chicago during those years, working on my master's in English. This was a time of groping to find our way through relaxed rules and freedom that we were unaccustomed to after many years of Germanic strictness. What I personally experienced was also what many other women and men religious were undergoing. We were all in this together and even gravitated toward each other in our new-found freedom. "It was the best of times; it was the worst of times."

At Loyola University's downtown campus was a piano bar across the street from the Student Union. It was not uncommon to be invited out for an evening of entertainment. The lake, theaters, restaurants on the lakeshore campus were also enticing attractions, to say nothing of the night clubs in Chicago. Night life prevailed; dating began. I saw elderly Jesuits shaking their heads in disbelief of what was happening all around them.

Several professors and priests invited me to join in the fun; however, I did not want them to look upon me as "an easy catch." Although I must say, several of these men were very appealing to me. When I saw the signs of "getting serious" and leading up to dating, I graciously declined.

Furthermore, Loyola's English department was noted for being tough. My primary goal was to do well in my classes and graduate. I had no time to engage in entertainment, let alone develop a relationship. In addition to that, my dad paid for my degree at Loyola so that if I ever left community, I would not be saddled with a debt to pay back. I saw how hard Mom and Daddy had worked and the sacrifices they made to educate us. No way was I going to squander the time with frivolity when I should be studying.

I think it was wholesome and healthy that religious communities and the Church went through these turbulent times, even though my religious community suffered a great loss in membership. My closest friends left community which was difficult for me to process. Thereafter, I asked myself many questions. Why am I staying? Should I leave when there is no stigma attached to leaving? Should I leave when I'm still in my childbearing years? Is this life really for me? What am I running away from and running to? Am I really happy as a nun? Is this the life where I can feel most fulfilled and make a difference? Is God still calling me to this life? In addition to all the tests I had at Loyola University, this was the personal examination I frequently took.

After much prayer and discernment, I made the decision to remain in community and have never regretted or felt I made a mistake. I blessed my friends for the choice they made.

Recently, a young lady considered entering our community. She was willing to take the vows of poverty and obedience, but did not want to embrace chastity. Sorry, lady! No *à la carte*!

Chapter VII
Teaching and Learning

After my first profession in 1952, I looked forward to staying at the motherhouse to continue pursuing a degree in music. September came and many principals and teachers in the community were preparing for the new school year. By that time, Mother Corona had made all the appointments, we thought.

The afternoon before the opening of school, Mother Corona called me to the office and said, "Sister, I'm sending you to Holy Redeemer School in Milwaukee to teach first grade. School begins tomorrow, I'm desperate for a teacher. Sister Arthur Minten is a master teacher and she will assist you. I know you can do it. The sisters will be here at 5:30 to get you."

What a curve ball that was! I had little time to respond, other than, "Yes, Mother." This was the first test of my vow of obedience. I ran down to the music department, and with tears in my eyes, kissed my violin and placed the case on the shelf. I packed up my music books and took them to the office. Quickly, I gathered my belongings and stuffed them in a suitcase. I met Sister Johannella Fiecke, the director of junior sisters. She looked at me with sadness in her eyes and said, "This is a difficult assignment, isn't it, but God is with you. Goodbye and blessings on your work." I had no time to say goodbye to anyone else. I was off!

I walked into the community room at Holy Redeemer Convent where 38 sisters were excited and making final preparations for school. Sister Stanisia Schmidt introduced me to the group. They were elated to see me. Sister Arthur immediately handed 48 paper crowns to me on which to print the students' names. I couldn't figure out why first graders needed crowns when I was concerned about books and materials for teaching. I soon found out that the crowns were to be worn by the children so that I could identify the students with their names.

Fortunately, Sister Arthur had already made the lesson plans for me and explained what I was to do. When I went to bed that night, I was filled with excitement and anxiety, a combination of emotions I had never experienced. In the past, it was always one or the other.

When 48 energetic students with happy faces entered the room that morning, they transformed me. I looked forward to the challenge of teaching them. And what a challenge it was after six years of being alone in a private music studio.

I followed the lesson plans methodically, and after two hours, I had completed all my tasks. I went to Sister Arthur and said, "I've finished the plans, so now what do I do?" She looked at me, smiled, and said, "Go back to your classroom and teach it all over again." She herself had 55 students and the other first grade teacher, 45. There was no time for her to explain what I should do for the rest of the day, especially since those plans were designed to last the entire day.

Fortunately, there was a piano in my classroom, so after I went through the lesson plans again, there still was time to spare. Toward the end of the day, the children became restless. What better solution to calm them down than teaching a song. What song? Gregorian Chant? The Star Spangled Banner? Ah! I quickly recalled a ditty I had learned in first grade. I squatted to the floor in my long habit and slowly rose to the ascending scale.

> I had a little puppy
> He had a stubby tail
> He wasn't very fat
> He was skinny as a rail
> But now my puppy's gone
> He no longer comes around
> They sell him at the butcher shop for 30 cents a pound.

By this time I was in an upright position and slowly descending to the floor, I sang

> Bow-wow-wow-wow—wow-wow-wow.

and jumped up on

> Hot Dogs!

The children loved it! Immediately without any instructions, 48 students squatted to the floor as I sang, and you can only imagine what a tumultuous sound it was when they jumped up to "hot dogs."

I did not realize the so-called "old church," which was still being used, was underneath my classroom. The new church was at the other end of the property. Father Joseph Fisher, one of the assistant pastors was making a Holy Hour. He came running up the stairway, charged into my room thinking some great catastrophe had happened.

I was embarrassed and apologetic, as the children in all sincerity asked if they could perform for Father and were already on the floor ready to start. They didn't even know the words to the song as yet, but everyone certainly knew "hot dogs." Father Fisher laughed aloud and left the room. With all the emphasis on animal rights, I'm sure the response today would be different. Probably many children would be in tears thinking of their own puppy becoming a hot dog.

After one week of trial and error, Mother Corona asked Sister Patrice McGlone, one of the community supervisors, to visit my classroom. That was a blessing. I was teaching manuscript at the blackboard. I then proceeded down the aisles to check on the children's work. When I saw Billy's paper, I said, "You can't syllabicate the word like this." He (Billy Bruckner) looked up at me and said, "What does 'sab-i-cate' mean?" That did it. After the lunch period, Sister Patrice in all kindness said, "Sister, I will teach your class and I want you to observe Sister Arthur for one week." That was all I needed! To see a model teacher set me on a new course. I still had my challenging moments, but nothing in comparison to what might have been.

Sister Avellino and first grade student, Billy Bruckner, Holy Redeemer School, Milwaukee, Wisconsin, 1953

Sister Arthur was delighted after several months to hear how well my students read. When I sent the pre-primers home with the children to read to their parents, one of the fathers called me in the evening and said, "I'm delighted to hear how well Jack reads with a southern accent." Perhaps that's why Sister Emanuella Bruschi nicknamed me "Magnolia Blossom" and thereafter, the sisters at Holy Redeemer Convent affectionately called me by that name.

My greatest difficulty was not teaching, but disciplining the children. I saw how Sister Arthur was firm, and yet kind. The children knew she loved them and they loved her. It took a semester for me to learn not to be too soft on those loveable human beings that wormed their way into my heart. Once I learned the techniques of firmness, such as disciplining with my eyes rather than raising my voice, I felt I had achieved one of the qualities of a good teacher. Amazingly so, what I learned in teaching first grade benefited me for my entire teaching career. I taught all grades through college and felt fulfilled and rewarded as a teacher.

As the end of the school year was fast approaching, I was tired and ready for a break. Sister Arthur was approaching retirement, a term not used in our community at that time. And by retirement, I mean she was already in her mid 70s and having health issues. She wanted to ease her load of teaching. At the end of the school year she said to me, "Now that you are doing well as a classroom teacher, I want you to take over some of my responsibilities next school year." I agreed to assist her in any way I could. I was now perfectly content to pursue classroom teaching as opposed to giving private music lessons in the future.

Our plans were derailed. Sister Stanisia received a call from Mother Corona one month before the next school year began. I was completing summer classes at Alverno College. She said, "Since Sister Avellino can now teach as well as play the organ and conduct a choir, I'm sending her to a new school that is opening in Warrenville, Illinois."

Another curve ball! Strike two! When Sister Stanisia informed me, she had tears in her eyes. I had grown to know and love the sisters at Holy Redeemer. She said, "Since you haven't played the organ for a year, you must start playing again, so tomorrow morning, you will play the seven o'clock Requiem Mass. I found out later that Sister Stanisia called Mother Corona and requested that I remain at Holy Redeemer. I felt as if I were playing my own Requiem. I cried during the whole Mass as three sisters sang. Father Fisher celebrated the Mass and kept looking back at the choir. He had never seen me on the organ bench.

I felt sorry for dear Sister Arthur. She was the one who invested time and energy in me so I could eventually spread my wings and fly. Saying goodbye to her was soul wrenching. She cried. I cried. The sisters gathered in the community room where I had first met them almost a year ago and waved their handkerchiefs in farewell to their "Magnolia Blossom."

We were charting new waters as Sisters Reginald Braunger, Altheus Schoenbauer, Clotilda Dahlman and I rang the rectory doorbell at St. Irene Parish in Warrenville. The pastor, Father Aloysius Stier said

to us, "You have come here as missionaries." I could not comprehend
that in a suburb of Chicago we were to be missionaries, but I soon

learned what the pastor meant. If I thought
Holy Redeemer was a challenge, St. Irene's far
exceeded it.

The convent was in the residential
part of the town, several blocks from the
church and school. Father drove us to our new
dwelling, gave us the keys, and went back to
the rectory. The convent was a modest house,
simply furnished with three bedrooms and a
bath upstairs, a kitchen, dining/living room,
and chapel on the first floor. There were also a
basement, a large enclosed porch, and a separate

Father Aloysius Stier

garage on the property, but at that time, we were not permitted to drive.

After attending Mass the next day with only two other people, the
priest's housekeeper and a gentleman, Sister Aletheus and I remained in
the church to check out the boys' sacristy. We saw hours of work staring
at us: the censer, candle holders, flower vases, cassocks, surpluses were
filthy. I walked up to the tabernacle to remove the dirty curtains and they

literally disintegrated. The
priests' sacristy also required
intense work. We knew now
why the pastor had built the
school, which was empty for
one year until he could get the
School Sisters of St. Francis
to staff it, because we were
the only order that did sacristy
work.

Then Sister Aletheus
and I walked to the modern
school built by architects Belli
and Belli. Each classroom had
one entire side of windows

St. Irene Convent on Fourth Street, 1960

from the ceiling to the floor. I loved it, the more windows; the more light.
We joined Sisters Reginald in the office to rearrange files. Sister Clotilda,
our domestic sister, returned to the convent after Mass to acclimate

herself to the kitchen and her new surroundings.

It was shocking to Sisters Reginald, Aletheus and me that no books had been ordered and there were no desks in the first grade classroom where I was to teach. We had only two weeks before school was to begin. Needless to say, Sister Reginald with our assistance went to the telephone and called publishing companies to rush orders we placed. I taught for an entire month without desks and books. Imagine 45 children sitting on the floor trying to learn with no books. Talk about a challenge! Thank God for the year I had with Sister Arthur!

I sent a note home with the children, asking the parents to come to my rescue. The next day they came with tablets, pencils, and crayons. At least that was a starter. The principal, Sister Wanda Kluthe, at the neighboring St. Michael's School in Wheaton, gave me a set of primary text books. Several days later, she delivered rhythm band instruments and a chair for me. I was now ready to begin teaching like I had never done before.

It is amazing what one can do when there are few other options. I was forced to be creative. My training in music was invaluable. I had the greatest rhythm band in the Joliet Diocese! This was not only a good experience for me, but for the children. We learned that much can be accomplished with few resources. When the desks and books finally arrived, we celebrated. I called Ruzicka's Drug Store to deliver Dixie cups for the children as a reward for their good behavior and eagerness to learn under these circumstances.

The year was difficult for all of us, including the lay teacher, Eleanor McCaffery. Opening a new school with all eight grades, and children coming from several public schools is something I would never advocate. It would have been much wiser to begin with four grades, then add a grade each year, but we had no input in the matter. We managed to keep our sanity.

After three months, Sister Reginald was diagnosed with TB and returned to Milwaukee for treatment. As though we didn't have enough to do, Sister Aletheus and I sterilized everything in the convent, and were grateful we had not gotten the disease.

The absence of a principal placed a great burden on the two of us until a replacement could be made. It was during this time that we decided to put on a musical show with the entire school, 110 children. I told Sister Aletheus I would teach the music and choreography if she and

Mrs. McCaffery would discipline the children. This was a great way to engage the student body.

We arranged chairs in the basement to accommodate all the grades and began our venture. I soon discovered that these unruly children had talent. They put their hearts and souls in music and acting. We proceeded with the show even though after a week, Mother Corona assigned Sister Adolphine Rittmann, a community supervisor, to take Sister Reginald's place. What was intended to be a temporary appointment ended up being for the entire year, which was a blessing. The combined talents and experiences of the three of us made St. Irene School the talk and pride of the town.

Now that the school was in shape, we concentrated on the parish. Very few people attended Mass and even fewer received communion. Father Stier said many of the people were invalidly married; consequently, they were not allowed to receive communion in the Catholic church. This disturbed me greatly. Some of these were parents of my students. I found them to be loving, responsible parents. Why does the Catholic church make them feel they are living in sin is a question I asked myself then, and now, and in my advanced age, I'm still asking the same question.

Sister Aletheus and I decided to walk each evening down the streets of Warrenville, even though we were not permitted to enter homes. In our subtle way, we were missionaries attempting to bring the people closer to God. What a great experience that was for the two of us. We began establishing relationships with people. Little by little, the children and their parents came out to greet and invite us into their homes. A number of people became converts. First Communion brought many parents back to the Church. Each year attendance at Mass increased. It was interesting as sacristan, who filled one small ciborium with hosts to be consecrated once a month, eventually progress to a large vessel that was filled every week.

I was fortunate to be in the parish for 16 years and see the fruits of our labor. Being the only sister of the original group, I was privileged to live in the convent built next to the school. Each of the sisters had a private bedroom and enjoyed the luxury of modern appliances. After I left the parish, a church was built, which accommodated the growth of the parish.

Father Stier, a wise and holy priest, often said, "If I had to start a new parish, I would first build a school, then the church, a convent and lastly, a rectory." Given the reality today with empty convents, and in some dioceses, priests no longer living in rectories, Father Stier would have to rethink his strategy. In fact, St. Irene Convent is used for parish offices today.

St. Irene Convent on the parish grounds
Back: Sisters Melanta Haky, Willetta Schaefers,
Bernhilde Walter
Front: Sisters Avellino Stiefermann and Charlette Yancik

When we Sisters first arrived in Warrenville, the town was unincorporated. About six years later, a group of professionals and business owners were strongly pushing for incorporation. Since I was teaching seventh grade at this time, I took the opportunity to instruct the students about incorporation and the process of establishing a city/town government. Elections were to be held soon, so, I too, advocated incorporating the town and taught the children the advantages.

That evening, the convent doorbell rang and Judge Edwin Douglas, a resident of Warrenville who worked in the Wheaton courthouse, handed a bottle of wine to me and said, "I want to thank you for teaching incorporation to the students." His daughter Diane was in the class, and apparently informed her dad about what I had taught.

Not all parents were as receptive. One irate parent reported me to our provincial, Mother Calestine Schwener, in Rockford, Illinois. On the day elections were being held, Mother Calestine called the convent and said that we may not vote because we don't pay taxes. I was appalled that she would deny us our right to vote, and I was angry. My superior, Sister Willetta Schaefers was willing to obey the command. I was not. I called the pastor and Stanley Girard, an influential businessman and parishioner, who was going to drive us to the polls. I informed them of what had happened and requested that they speak to Mother Calestine, which they did. She then called the convent and said, "You may vote, but don't all of you go to the polls at once." I could live with that. It just meant that Mr. Girard had to make more than one trip, or we would have to ask another parishioner to drive us.

When I arrived at the polls, an aggressive middle-aged man stood before me and said, "You may not vote!" I abruptly walked around him and said, "I am an American citizen. You cannot deny me the right to vote!" With that I slipped into the voting booth. When I left the booth, two Cenacle Sisters were being given the same treatment. I saw them push their way to the booth and vote.

To my delight, Warrenville became incorporated. Ironically, months later, I was asked to run for alderwoman. One thousand signatures had already been received. I declined because I "do not pay taxes." At that time, the order did not allow us to run for public office. I did lead the opening prayer and attended City Council meetings, until it was too difficult to juggle my parish duties.

My responsibilities in the parish were many: full-time teacher, organist, choir director, and sacristan. It seems incomprehensible today that I did all this for $90 a month, and $25 for organ and choir work. Unfortunately, because I was overworked, my health began to suffer. For five years, I dealt with a condition known as achalasia of the esophagus, where no food went directly into my stomach. I had a constriction of the esophagogastric junction. In order for food to get to the stomach, I ate until my esophagus filled to the point of choking. Then I ran to the bathroom and drank glasses of water quickly. The pressure of water slowly opened the gastric junction that slowly closed again. Whatever food succeeded in getting into my stomach during that brief interval was my meal, unless I chose to repeat this process five more times to get down a full meal. The food and water remaining in the esophagus had to be regurgitated each time before I could begin the process over again.

When eating in public, I ate only to the point of not choking. The food stayed lodged in my esophagus until I discreetly found a place where I could drink glasses of water and regurgitate. In view of my responsibilities, I was often in public and somehow managed to cover up my condition.

The most discouraging factor about this affliction was that no doctor at that time knew how to treat it. I went to many doctors, including a cardiologist who said I had the strongest heart in DuPage County. I was finally sent to our community hospital in Waupun,

Wisconsin, where I spent an entire summer. Six doctors held a staff meeting regarding my condition. I listened to each doctor express different diagnoses with the final word from the chief of staff who wanted to do exploratory surgery. I strongly objected and said to the doctors, "When you cut me open, you're not to remove anything, or insert anything into me. You have to do something to get my system to function properly. Surgery is not going to work." I refused to sign the papers.

The director of nurses reported me to Mother Corona as being "a young, obstinate sister who refused to take the suggestion of the chief of staff." She called me at the hospital the next day. I explained what had happened and what I had said, and then put the question to her: "Mother Corona, would you sign the papers if six doctors each had a different diagnosis and wanted to do an exploratory?" She said, "No." The matter was dismissed. Obviously, the doctors were not happy with me. They prescribed Pro-Banthine to relieve spasms and said I should remain at the hospital for observation. I later learned from the specialist who did finally cure me one year later that this drug made the condition worse. The specialist also said that the smartest thing I did was refuse to sign the papers for exploratory surgery. A man from Texas had three-fourths of his stomach removed, another patient had removal of a portion of the esophagus, both ending up with the same original problem. Surgery was not the answer.

When I left the hospital, the chief of staff said to me, "I never want to see you again in this hospital." I replied, "Doctor, you will never again see me in this hospital, but when I'm cured, you will receive a letter from me." After I was cured, I wrote a lengthy letter to the chief of staff but never received a response.

I prayed, as did my parents and the sisters with whom I lived, that I would someday find a doctor who could cure me. Each day I prayed, "Lord, if I could just touch the hem of your garment, I know I would be healed." Only my strong faith and the grace of God helped me through this difficult time.

I also give thanks each day for the gift of water. Were it not for this precious gift, I could never have lived. It disturbs me greatly to see how we take water for granted in our country today. The waste and pollution are alarming. The thought often occurs to me that eventually, with the climate changes we are experiencing, water may someday be "gold." Think about it. We may be on our knees praying Psalm 63.

> My soul thirsts for you,
> my body longs for you
> in this dry and weary land where there is no water.

I returned to St. Irene's to begin another school year. It's amazing that I continued teaching and performing my other duties all during this traumatic time. The pastor and parishioners never were aware of my problem, for which I was grateful.

I was very thin, and actually could not afford to lose weight. The habit somewhat disguised my body weight. Because I looked healthy and was still active, some doctors thought it was "all in my head." I knew better.

I went to Mother Clemens Rudolph who was assistant to Mother Corona. I told her of my condition and said that I would not take Perpetual Vows if I were not cured because of the difficulty living a communal life. She did not want me to leave the community. Her immediate response was encouraging, "Sister, we will do everything to help you find the right doctor. I will write a note to Doctor Barnes at our Sacred Heart Sanitarium to have x-rays taken."

This was good news to me. I had previously gone to him, and he, as well as other doctors, would not x-ray me because I looked healthy and they felt I had some mental problem. Doctor Barnes still remembered me, but at the request of Mother Clemens, ordered the x-rays, which were taken on a Saturday.

Doctor Barnes was at his home raking leaves when the radiologist called him to come immediately to the sanitarium. When he arrived, I was sitting on the x-ray machine, and he came and sat beside me. Putting his arms around me, and with teary eyes, he said, "Sister, I am so sorry I misjudged you. Your esophagus is much larger than your stomach. I do not know how to treat your condition, but I will search the world for a doctor to help you."

One year later, Doctor Baburka came from Vienna to Chicago's Northwestern University. Doctor Barnes had made an appointment and informed me of the day and the hour. "Be sure you're there at this precise time; he's only here for three days," he said. Nothing would prevent me from going!

When I arrived at Passavant Hospital, Doctor Baburka said to me, "You don't look as if you have cancer. If this is not cancer, I can cure you." He ordered x-rays and other tests. The next morning this renowned doctor, who had received an award from Pope Pius XII for outstanding work in the medical field, came bouncing into my room like an athlete. "I can cure you! I can cure you! It's not cancer!" What a relief! Even the sisters with whom I lived and my family had thought I had cancer. Then he said, "I'm retiring, so I will entrust you to a doctor I have trained. He will take good care of you." He shook hands with me, wished me well and said goodbye.

Within an hour, Doctor Clinton E. Texter walked into my room as I sat in a chair clad in full habit. After introducing himself to me, he said, "I'm taking you to a classroom at Northwestern University where 18 doctors are waiting for us. There is no place for you to undress over there, so I will ask a nurse to find a uniform for you." With that, he left the room.

Shortly thereafter, in walked a nurse with a fresh, crisp uniform and placed it on the bed. "I think this will fit you," she said, "and just hang all your clothes in the closet." I quickly undressed and donned the nurse's uniform. Within a short time, Dr. Texter came back to my room. "Come with me," he said as we went down the corridor, down the elevator and across the street to Northwestern University. I noticed the people we met all but bowed to this doctor.

I felt life-threatened as I walked into a large room with 18 doctors, some of whom were foreign, staring at me. I soon realized that these were doctors who were there to learn from Doctor Texter how to treat my illness. I was relieved to know that after all the torture and misunderstandings I had encountered, that there would be future doctors knowledgeable about this condition. I was willing to submit myself to any treatment to advance medical knowledge.

Doctor Texter had me lie down on a large table and told the doctors to gather around. He began explaining the constriction and that he was going to test the peristaltic movements of the esophagus and then calculate how many centimeters to dilate the esophagogastric junction. In order to do this, he attached wires to my body. A huge screen covering an entire wall registered what was going on with my esophagus. I had no idea of the medical interpretation of what appeared as lines, dots and dashes as I was lying in a horizontal position. I remained still and prayed to all the angels and saints to surround me and the doctor.

Doctor Texter allowed students to assist him with attaching the wires. All of a sudden, he literally grabbed a wire from the hands of a student saying, "You are going to electrocute her!" I was terrified and grabbed Doctor Texter's arm and said, "Doctor, don't you dare let any other doctor touch me." I noticed the imprints of my fingernails still present in his arm the next day. Doctor Texter was very apologetic as the other doctors became like statues standing around the table. There was a long silence as he allowed me to gain composure so he could proceed with the testing. At that moment, I felt the entire heavenly court was above and around me. I prayed to Christ the Healer to guide and direct Doctor Texter.

The next day I was taken to the x-ray department for the dilatation of the esophagogastric junction. The room was dark. I sat on a chair. A young American doctor came up to me and said, "You can swallow this, can't you?" I looked at this round cylinder, the length of a knife, attached to a green garden hose with a syringe at the end. In disbelief I said, "Yes, I can swallow it." In the meantime, I saw Doctor Texter pacing nervously back and forth in front of the room. To say the least, this frantic back and forth made me feel uneasy about the procedure that was about to happen.

The American doctor said, "If you can synchronize your breathing with the rhythm of my putting this down your throat, it will be much easier to swallow." The team work was terrific! In three minutes I could feel the Mosher dilator go through the constriction. Doctor Texter was utterly shocked that I did not once gag. He said, "Sister, you should be a sword swallower." In two previous male patients, it had taken three hours to accomplish what we did in three minutes.

I was then placed on a fluoroscope machine. Doctor Texter approached me and said, "Sister, this is the most torturous treatment for any human being. I regret I cannot sedate you, but if you hang in there and not move, you will be cured." The word "cure" was music to my ears. He then explained what he was going to do. "I will squeeze the syringe three times, then six, nine, and finally twelve. So let's begin." I prayed that I could endure the pain as I lay frozen waiting to be healed. Out of nowhere, another doctor appeared on the other side of the fluoroscope machine. Judging from his role as the procedure began, I assumed he was a psychiatrist.

Dr. Texter said, "I'm going to squeeze the syringe three times

now," and he counted aloud, in a steady rhythm—one, two, three."
Torture it was! Then he handed the syringe to the American doctor and
said, "Now we will inflate the Mosher dilator six times—one, two, three,
four, five, six." I felt like Joan of Arc being burnt at the stake. The pain
was excruciating! The psychiatrist was like a cheerleader, "Sister, you're
doing great! You are the most courageous woman I've met. Hang in
there, You're going to make it to the finish line." The syringe was then
handed to the psychiatrist, and to the rhythmic count by Doctor Texter
was blown up nine times. I thought I would die as I heard, "Sister, you
are fantastic! You are the greatest woman!" Then for the final twelve
counts, Doctor Texter said, "This is the worst pain I could inflict on
anyone," as tears rolled down his cheeks. His voice softened as he
counted to twelve. Thank God. I had reached the finish line. The doctors
were as excited as little boys. I heard Doctor Texter say, "It's a perfect
dilatation! Perfect dilatation!"

I then went to an adjacent room to swallow barium as they
observed me standing in an upright position through the fluoroscope
machine. When I felt the barium go directly into my stomach, the
exhaustion and emotional response were so profound that I fell off the
machine, hitting Doctor Texter, who spilled the barium he was holding,
and I landed on the floor. The doctors called on the nurses to assist at
this point. They could not get me to come to as they all knelt on the floor
trying to revive me. I have no idea how long I was in this state. I was
shocked when I did revive to see everyone hovering around me on the
floor. I was so weak that I could not stand up without assistance. Seeing
how weak I was, the psychiatrist picked me up and carried me to the
cart. The American doctor then took me to my room and assisted me into
bed. Doctor Texter came to the room about an hour later. By this time I
started to cry and cry. I could not stop. Doctor Texter held my hand and
said, "I would be greatly disturbed if you did not cry. Two men I had
previously dilated cried for at least three hours. You are the first woman
I've treated, and truthfully, I was apprehensive that you would even live
through this procedure."

I cried and cried and finally said, "Thank you, thank you. Doctor
Texter—next to God." Those words must have stunned him. I later
learned that he was an atheist. Whether or not that is true, I don't know.
If it is, who takes God more seriously than an atheist?

When it was time for the evening meal, Doctor ordered a steak.

I hadn't eaten a steak for years, so I was fearful when I took the first swallow as he sat observing me. I couldn't believe that it went through the esophagogastric junction into the stomach. This seemed abnormal to me; I had accepted my previous condition as normal.

Doctor Texter, still doing research, returned to my room the next day with a book he had written on achalasia and asked me to read and critique it. He was eager to learn from me any additional information that he may have omitted and to comment on inaccuracies. He later thanked me for the contributions I made. On this same note, Doctor Texter was to conduct a World Congress in Munich, Germany, six months later. He said, "I would deeply appreciate if you could go with me and be a part of this event." When I asked Mother Corona for permission, her response was, "You are going to Germany with a doctor? No." I was disappointed in her reply. It was another occasion when the vow of obedience was difficult to observe. I think she was more concerned about my vow of chastity and whether or not I would persevere as a sister, especially since I had not yet taken perpetual vows. Who knows what may have happened?

Today, I would not have had to ask permission. I would make my own decision and choose to inform leadership where I am going and why. I am sure that our leaders today would say "yes" to this request.

Doctor Texter gave some good advice to me as he sat by my bedside.

> You can live a long life now that you are cured of this illness, but you must heed Nature's warning signal. Very few people have a built-in signal as you have now with your esophagus, which will warn you when you are over stressed. Listen to your body. Your body does not lie.

> You need to make some changes in your life, which I know you will do. After this significant disruption in your journey, you will see reality from a new perspective. Make sure you have emotional outlets. Do activities that make you happy. You can't have all work and no play.

I realized I was working morning, noon, and night and had to make some changes. I was also a perfectionist and demanded perfection from others, which was not only stressful to myself, but often to others. Thus, I returned to St. Irene Parish having learned many lessons, especially in treating my body with reverence and care. I was forced to create balance in my life.

Doctor Texter had a twinkle in his eyes when he said, "Had you taken a glass of wine each evening with your meal when you first felt this coming on, you probably could have avoided getting a constriction. Be grateful that you have learned at a young age the price that is paid when you do not listen to your body."

Years later when I was in Paris visiting friends, the Parisians raised their glasses of wine each evening and toasted one another with "à votre santé"—to your health. To you the readers, I raise my glass of Pinot Noir—"à votre santé."

Chapter VIII
Adventures in Ministries

After being cured of achalasia of the esophagus, I returned to St. Irene Parish energized and renewed. Sisters Adria Hrabovsky, principal, Charlette Yancik, Christoval Meyer, and Mary Shawn O'Brien eagerly awaited my return. I was in Passavant Hospital six days, and was cured in 45 minutes, which seemed miraculous after having gone five years with this dreadful affliction. Sister Bernhilde Walter, our domestic sister, prepared a candlelight dinner with my favorite foods and Pinot Gregio wine as a toast to me. What a great welcome from the sisters who patiently and lovingly tolerated my exits from the table to the bathroom for five years!

Besides the sisters, two lay teachers were hired on the faculty: Patricia Rovai and Veronica Corbeil. I continued with my previous responsibilities determined to pace myself and deal with stress. I was the youngest person on the faculty and craved more physical activities, so I took time for meditative nature walks, wined and dined with friends, and

St. Irene School Faculty
Sisters Adria Hrabovsky, principal, Christoval Meyer, Charlette Yancik,
Avellino, Bernhilde Walter

had fun teaching a group of students baton twirling. My long habit was no hindrance.

From day one, Warrenville was an interesting town in which to live. I never knew what to expect; consequently, I learned to appreciate each moment as it came and realized the sacredness of the unexpected. I met some intriguing and inspiring people while teaching at St. Irene's. Two persons in particular; namely Donald Jansen, a student, and Father Michael Sawlewicz, assistant priest, had a great impact on my life. Their compelling stories are covered in the next two chapters.

Living in the residential part of town rather than in a convent on parish grounds, offered different experiences. Behind our convent was a yard and at the end of the property were large trees and shrubbery hiding a log cabin. The neighbors informed us that a prominent lawyer who had never lost a case in the Chicago courts lived in this cabin. Apparently, after having lost a court battle, he could not accept defeat, so he became a recluse and miser. We sisters often saw him in the cold of winter walking down the street with newspapers wrapped around his legs, a torn jacket and a tattered old hat going to the corner grocery store to purchase milk and bread. None of the neighbors had ever spoken to him or visited him, although they were able to identify him as Mr. Moore.

Our domestic Sister Theresita Skolaski made wonderful bread each week. She suggested we place a loaf of homemade bread at his doorstep, knowing he would never answer the door. I was elected to trot across the backyard and squeeze through the shrubs to carry out our mission. The good thing was that the loaf disappeared each week which meant he stepped out of his cabin to pick it up. Only once did he open the door wide enough that I could see a bush growing inside on the dirt floor. As a Franciscan with the vow of poverty, I would leave his place feeling "this is real poverty."

Once a year, Mr. Moore dressed in a black suit and tall black hat to attend a printer's convention in Chicago. He had been a professional printer at one time. Father Stier told us of an occasion a lady sitting next to him on the Aurora Elgin Train said, "Sir, you smell" to which he replied, "Lady, you smell; I stink."

Between him and the famous Albright brothers, Malvin and Ivan, who were artists and lived a similar lifestyle in Warrenville, I had plenty to amuse, interest, and inspire me. Ivan Albright had been commissioned to paint the aged and corrupt portrait of Dorian Gray. When the

Hollywood producers came to Warrenville to check on his progress, Ivan and Malvin were found drunk in a ditch. Ivan increased his price when a deadline was placed upon him. The oil painting has been displayed in the Art Institute of Chicago since 2011.

Weekly, I made my jaunt to the log cabin. On Christmas Eve, the convent doorbell rang. I answered the door. To my surprise, there stood Mr. Moore with a shabby hat and jacket and newspapers wrapped around his legs. I invited him in our enclosed porch, and then into the living room. "Oh no Mam, I would never enter your living room," he said.

I saw him gently reach into his pocket and take out a little toy dish. It was gold-colored, caked with mud and cracked. Placing it tenderly in both his hands, he reached out as his penetrating, blue eyes looked at me, and said, "Lady, this is just a little token of my gratitude for all that you ladies have done for me." What a Christmas gift! Mr. Moore, the recluse, stepped out of his comfort zone to thank us. That little dish was placed on our altar as a symbol of giving and gratitude. Christmas was special for us that year.

Mr. Moore died. Nieces and nephews, who had never come to see or check up on him, ransacked the log cabin and found an enormous amount of cash in the cracks and crevices. This poor man was a millionaire.

After 14 years at St. Irene Parish, Mother Clemens sent me to St. Alexis Parish in Bensenville, Illinois. I was open and happy to have a change; however, I was apprehensive about the reason I was being transferred there. The pastor, Father Matthew Kauth, was unhappy with the organist and choir and had requested a change. This German pastor loved music and set high expectations on the choir director. In addition to music, I was to teach fifth grade. My first thought was am I going to meet his expectations. Would I be any better than my predecessor? Momentarily, I lost my confidence.

When I arrived in Bensenville, I was jarred by the airplanes taking off at O'Hare Field and zooming uncomfortably low over the parish complex. Every three minutes a plane cast its shadow as it flew over the school and church. My first nights in that convent I was unable to sleep as planes roared overhead. How will I ever survive in this parish, let alone teach music? Amazingly, after several weeks, the sounds of airplanes actually lulled me to sleep.

During the homily at Mass, the priests could not compete

with the rumbling sounds so they often remained silent until the noise subsided. The same was true with my teaching. Needless to say, we had many reflective moments of silence. The parishioners, faculty, and students had already adapted to this situation. I had to adjust to circumstances that could not be changed.

The first Sunday I was at St. Alexis, I attended Mass at which the women's choir sang. I sat in the congregation and listened. What a distraction! How could anyone worship with this kind of music? The associate pastor, Father Patrick O'Sullivan, in his Irish brogue, called the women "cackling hens."

When I spoke to him, I said, "Father, you need to help get people to join the choir. Please put an ad in the parish bulletin for men and women, and even high school and college students, if they are willing to make a commitment." Father O'Sullivan was as eager as I to develop a good choir.

We received a wonderful response from parishioners. And to my surprise and delight, Father, with all his Irish charisma, succeeded in recruiting male and female singers from Fenton High School's acapella choir.

The choir loft was spacious enough to accommodate 75 singers. We ended up with 50, which made me happy. I asked the lay organist to continue playing and said to the 10 ladies that we were expanding the choir, and in order not to hurt their feelings, they could remain or choose to leave. Half left, and with training, I was comfortable with those who chose to continue.

I worked diligently with the choir and enjoyed hearing the blend and balance that improved with each rehearsal. The members were cooperative and eager to become a choir of excellence. In addition to preparing for the Sunday High Masses, my goal was to have a beautiful liturgy for Christmas Midnight Mass. That was accomplished. After the Solemn High Mass with Father Kauth as celebrant, and Fathers O'Sullivan and Michael Lyons, as concelebrants, the pastor climbed the many steps in the back of the church to the choir loft. Given his heart condition, Father Kauth was short of breath and perspiring when he approached me while I was still seated on the organ bench. With tears in his eyes he said, "I thought I was in heaven tonight. The music was beautiful! Thank you, Sister."

Word soon circulated in the Joliet Diocese that St. Alexis had a good choir. In the fall, parishes prepared to implement the mandates of Vatican II on the first Sunday of Advent. Bishop Romeo Blanchette divided the diocese into four sections with a center training place in each area. Father O'Sullivan and I were appointed to train the cantors, lectors, musicians, and priests of the surrounding parishes.

Switching from Latin to English and priests having to face the congregation when celebrating Mass were challenges. For many priests, especially older ones, the change was traumatic. I learned later that a number of them took tranquilizers and/or had recourse to alcohol when celebrating Mass for the first time facing the people.

Shortly after Vatican II went into effect, Father Kauth became ill and died rather unexpectedly. This saddened the parishioners and was a great loss to me. Anything I had requested to enhance the music at St. Alexis, he granted. I loved and admired this priest who had a great sensitivity to beauty, not just for music, but even in the landscaping of the parish grounds. Each year he personally had planted thousands of petunias on his days off and made one feel the church and convent were in a botanical garden.

Every year on the feast of St. Nicholas, Father Kauth, portrayed as the saint, went to school and personally gave an apple, orange, and candy bar to each of the 560 children. What fond memories the children had of this priest.

For his funeral, I planned the music at quick notice and called the choir for rehearsals. Father O'Sullivan came to rehearsal crying, and said, "I feel I have lost my father. When I came from Ireland, Father Kauth was so kind to me. Let's give him a great send-off." And that we did.

The Mass was celebrated in English with Bishop Blanchette and many priests robed in white vestments instead of black. The church was filled with parishioners, family and friends who mourned the loss of their beloved pastor. Flowers decked the altars and the vestibule of the church. The choir sang with unusual artistry that day. It was truly a festive celebration of Father Kauth's life and his entrance into eternal life. I received numerous notes and comments later from priests and laity that the celebration was meaningful and beautiful in English. It was a manifestation of what Vatican II had initiated and the people's positive response.

Within several months, a new pastor was assigned to St. Alexis

Parish. Adapting to a new priest who was strikingly different than Father Kauth was a big adjustment for everyone. In all probability, it must have been difficult for the new pastor to transition to St. Alexis Parish.

As choir director, I had little contact with the new pastor. I was grateful that I had had one year under Father Kauth to develop a good choir and prepare the parish for Vatican II changes that were well in place. However, this feeling of peaceful sailing was of short duration.

On Sunday morning, as I sat on the organ bench facing the front of the church listening to Father Lyons' homily, my star bass singer discreetly came and sat beside me. What's this all about, I wondered. "Sister, I have something important I want to say to you. I belong to a gang in Chicago and next Sunday we plan to rob some churches and St. Alexis is one of them," Steve said in a calm, convincing voice. I was stunned. Steve, a member of a gang? Robbery? My immediate response was,

"Thank you for letting me know, but what do you want me to do with this knowledge?"

"Do with this information whatever you want; just know the robbery will happen," Steve said. "You have one week to prepare."

My next question was, "Are there any other gang members in this choir?"

His answer, "Oh, no!"

Again, I thanked him for telling me, and then said, "Steve, this means you will no longer be a member of this choir," which was difficult to say, because he was my best and most faithful bass singer. In a quivering voice I said, "Thank you for the great asset you've been. I will miss you, Steve. I pray and trust that you will chart a new path for yourself." With that he squeezed my hand; his eyes held tears.

By this time, the homily was completed and Father Lyons began the Creed and the congregation joined in the proclamation of faith. My thoughts, far removed from the Creed, were focused on telling the pastor about the impending robbery. The choir members sensed something was wrong. I tried my best to silence my thoughts. I was relieved when the priest gave the final blessing and said, "The Mass is ended. Go in peace to love and serve the Lord."

I did not leave the church in "peace." When I arrived at the convent, I told the superior, Sister Alfred Maluck, what had transpired during Mass. She did not welcome the news. The persons counting the collection each Sunday did so in the convent basement, which we assumed would be under tight security the next Sunday.

On Monday morning, after the seven o'clock Mass, I, in fear and trepidation, walked into the priests' sacristy as the pastor was removing his vestments. What I had anticipated happened. He exploded! "You get rid of all those young punks on the choir! And I don't ever want to see that cantor Tom up in the sanctuary again. I don't trust him! I don't trust any of them. Get rid of them, or I will."

I listened; I prayed. "Father, let's be grateful that Steve has given us a week's notice to prepare for the robbery," I said in a calm voice. "And I refuse to get rid of the so-called 'young punks' in the choir. They have done nothing wrong and have been faithful in coming to every rehearsal and Sunday Mass," I firmly asserted. Our retorts bounced back and forth like a ping-pong ball until I finally said, "Father, get rid of me and maybe your problems would be solved."

After a melodramatic silence, he said, "Leave!" I left confused: Was I to leave the sacristy, or leave the parish? I continued playing the organ and teaching fifth grade and wondered all week what was to happen.

Sunday morning came and to the utter dismay of parishioners, neighbors, and sisters, the premises were surrounded with police cars at all the Masses. Policemen here, policemen there, policemen everywhere! When I walked up to the choir, I was alarmed to see a policeman huddled in a corner of the loft. Is this for real? Am I hallucinating?

The choir members one by one took their places—no questions asked, but questions registered all over their faces. The Mass began with Father O'Sullivan as celebrant. I was relieved that it was not the pastor. Considering the circumstances, the choir sang exceedingly well. Steve was conspicuous by his absence, and the bass section did well without him.

To say the least, one could feel the tension throughout the congregation. Father O'Sullivan tried to give some comic relief during his homily and succeeded in getting the people to laugh. After the Mass was over, I played a lively postlude as people left the church wondering what was the meaning of this melodrama on this Sunday morning.

What did happen? St. Alexis Parish was not robbed. The gang members successfully robbed another church, and were caught *en route* to the next parish. Apparently, our pastor had alerted the neighboring parishes to take precautions. I said a prayer of thanksgiving that this daymare was over.

What happened to Steve? I wish I knew. I never saw or heard from him since he sat on the organ bench that Sunday morning. We missed Steve and often wished that we could have had more time to help him change and shape his destiny.

Did I get rid of the "young punks?" No. Did Father get rid of me? No. I was in the parish for only two years and then was sent back to St. Irene Parish to begin a dual enrollment program with the public school. Mother Ametista Steffen, provincial of the Rockford Province, assigned me there because I had already established good public relations with the people, and felt I would be a good team person to work with Richard Davis, the superintendent of public schools.

When I informed the pastor of St. Alexis I was leaving the parish, he shook hands with me and thanked me for what I had done for the parish. I was surprised to hear him say, "We will miss you," and "I wish you well at your new parish." I sensed a note of sadness in his face and voice, and even regret.

I went back to St. Irene Parish as principal and organist for five years. It was exciting to return to the parish where I had begun as a missionary and witness the growth and vitality of people deeply rooted in Christian values.

Working with Mr. Davis in the public school was a new and interesting challenge. The seventh and eighth grade students at St. Irene's attended Holmes School, walking distance, for science where they had labs and more equipment. I preferred having someone else teach science

St. Irene School Children's Choir, 1968

since there were times in the past that my experiments failed and my brightest students taught me and the class.

One of the great advantages of working with a superintendent who happened to be Jewish is that we collaborated in making purchases for both schools. I learned from him that one need not pay the amount listed on the price tag. He was shrewd and a competent business man who rarely paid the listed price. Because dual enrollment was a new and an experimental trend in education, Mr. Davis and I had many speaking engagements to public and private school educators.

Sister Barbaralie playing piano, 1970

I soon learned that the success of this program depended upon the personalities involved. While Mr. Davis and I were the administrators, dual enrollment was successful. Students learned and were happy; so were their parents. When Mr. Davis and I left Warrenville, it fell apart. Dual enrollment was short-lived, not only in Warrenville. Enrollment in the Catholic school suffered. Some parents resented paying tuition when their child was also in the public school, so why not enroll full time there?

Change was not only prevalent in education. In the mid 60s, my religious community was seriously involved in renewal of religious life. When I was in Bensenville, we still wore the long habit, but modified the collar and headdress with our hair showing. That was bad enough! The students who made bets that I had blonde hair soon saw that I was a brunette. We went through another greater change when I was in Warrenville; namely, our skirts were shortened to street length.

I wore the habit with great pride and dignity but welcomed the change, as did many sisters. As a result of having my head all bound up, my right ear became ulcerated. I went to three specialists, each of whom said my ear had to be amputated, which I refused to do. They insisted that I "get rid of the head gear." For one entire year, I removed the veil after teaching, bathed my ear several times a day, and applied

Sister Barbaralie, Rome, 1970

surgery powder. And there were times the pain was so severe, I went without the veil. Fortunately, I still have my ear. Other sisters suffered from drainage and corns on the ears.

Many sisters were anemic as a result of little exposure to the sun. Others suffered from prickly heat during the summer months. Some doctors who removed brain tumors from the sisters attributed them to the head gear. For medical reasons alone, the attire of the Middle Ages had to give way to a more modern style compatible to women of our times and culture.

The habit also disguised our womanly features and femininity. Showing our figures was supposedly not conducive to humility and virginity. The habit was another way of suppressing our sexuality. Now that most sisters dress in modern attire, the uniformity and conformity of the military model are history. Diversity in unity and unity in diversity herald the women religious of the 21st century.

You cannot imagine what this change was for us and our publics. Some thought all hell had broken loose! After being accustomed to seeing us as women in Middle Ages dress, it was a shock to see us modernize by showing our legs. I remember seeing a photo on the front page of several newspapers of a Sister of Mercy dressed in full habit, and next to it, the same sister dressed in a short skirt with fashion boots. The cutline beneath read, "You've come a long way baby!" Need I write more? The turbulent sixties passed and we survived.

The sensation of my new attire did not escape the people in Warrenville. The pastor thought I was leaving the convent. I was featured in the May 9, 1968, *Warrenville Digest* as a fashion model.

Our column is honored this week by having as its guest and model St. Irene's charming Sister Barbaralie. (Barbaralie Stiefermann). Her new black costume with its white cowl collar and white carnation for accent is the essence of smartness and becomingness too. The modern habit, by the way, was designed for her right here in Warrenville.

I marvel at the energy of this dedicated woman who is not only concerned as principal with many details of administration, and as eighth grade teacher with the instruction and moral guidance of youngsters in the precarious teens but also gives unsparingly of herself in those areas of community life where she can be most useful.

On the creative side, Sister Barbaralie is an accomplished musician, deeply interested in art and literature, and would love, if she had time, she tells me, to write poetry. After she was graduated from Alverno College, she attended DePaul, and more recently Loyola University where she is working for an additional master's degree in advanced studies in literature.

The Well Dressed Women of Warrenville

Their interests and activities

Sketched From Life

MILDRED BALDWIN

During Easter Week, Sister Barbaralie attended the National Catholic Education Convention in San Francisco where she deeply enjoyed the panoramic beauties of that golden city. She also visited the Haight-Ashbury district of the Hippies referred to in her article in this issue.

Though I write about fashion, I am less concerned with externals than with the spirit of the person I meet as a model, in this case, Sister Barbaralie whose warmth and whose precious gift of laughter constitute her special charisma.

The five years as principal at St. Irene's were exciting, challenging, and enterprising, but there were also tremendous difficulties. Within that time, there were two pastors, both of whom had serious problems, which greatly affected the parish and school. I was often the target for their weaknesses, insecurities, and incompetencies. When the problems escalated and became the bishop's responsibility, I was admonished: "In holy obedience do not make a fiasco at Mass." In 1971, I was removed from the parish and hired over the telephone by the principal, Mr. James O'Donnell at St. Francis High School in the neighboring town of Wheaton. He had knowledge of what had happened at St. Irene Parish. Three years later, while I was teaching at St. Francis High School, the bishop finally realized both pastors needed to be sent away for help. Bishop Blanchette apologized to me.

Fortunately, this was the time that I no longer had to be appointed by the provincial of my religious order. I was free to choose my place of work and living. I informed Sister Celestine Schall, provincial successor of Sister Ametista, of my decision to teach at St. Francis High School and live with the Wheaton Franciscans. She gave her blessing, knowing what had transpired previously.

Sister Barbaralie, principal, St. Irene School, and student, Linda Foote, 1968

St. Francis High School, at one time a prestigious school, was in a state of decline when I arrived there, due primarily to the changes in religious life. The principal was a former Christian Brother, as were several of the teachers. The Christian Brothers, noted for their teaching,

Sister Barbaralie, yearbook moderator and Sheila Cronin, St. Francis High School, 1976

had gone from strictness to a more relaxed lifestyle, as most religious orders experienced in the mid 60s and 70s. This was a time of confusion, adjustment, and chaos for men and women religious. This was a time of exodus from religious orders. Consequently, the lack of discipline, learning, cleanliness, building upkeep, and deplorable financial status were external manifestations of decadence at St. Francis High School, which was located in DuPage County—an area of affluence.

I found it difficult to transition from being a principal where I had discipline and academic excellence to "anything goes mentality." Several IBVM Sisters (Institute of the Blessed Virgin Mary), who were also members of the faculty, were my lifesavers. They were accustomed to teaching in girls' academies and found the situation discouraging, and yet, assured me, "Sister, this is not the way high schools normally function. We're so sorry this has to be your first experience in high school." At the end of the first semester, after a disgraceful student assembly, one of the sisters terminated her contract.

Father Anthony De Filippis, principal, St. Francis High School

The following year, Bishop Blanchette appointed three diocesan priests to assume leadership: Father Anthony DeFillipis, principal, Father Gerald Riva, religion and drama teacher, and Father Martin Gable, counselor and chaplain. Policies were established; rules were enforced. Not only students, but teachers also resisted the changes. The regulations appeared to be severe because there was too much indifference and freedom before. Father DeFillipis, to his credit, charged forth and did not waver in his intent to make this a Catholic school of excellence. He was small in stature and called "Little Caesar" by the students and affectionately by some people "Father D."

Sister Barbaralie, St. Francis High School, English

I went to my sophomore English class one morning and three-fourths of the students were absent. I knew something was up! I went to Father D and explained the situation. The two of us came to the conclusion that the students went to the home of parents who were vacationing in Hawaii. Father D said, "I'm going right to the house and chase them back to school." You can only imagine the shock of the students who were enjoying a champagne brunch when Father appeared in their midst. For the rest of the school year, these students

91

had to appear at St. Francis High School every Saturday at 9:00 a.m., shake hands with Father and clean the floors, windows, shine doorknobs, rake leaves, and pick up debris on the premises. Father supervised them and when they finished at noon, they shook hands with him again and had to say, "Thank you, Father." The students in the end gained respect for him and became friends. As for myself, when the students returned to the classroom, I said, "I'm really disappointed you didn't invite me to the champagne brunch." Years later, I was invited to the wedding of one of these students, who married later in life. The groom, as well as many of his classmates, raised their champagne glasses: "To Sister Barbaralie, who wasn't invited to our champagne brunch."

St. Francis High School Tour to Ireland, England, Wales, 1975. Bunratty Castle in Ireland for Medieval Feast Father Gerald Riva, Lord of the Castle; Sister Barbaralie, Lady of the Castle

At the end of the year, high school students are wild. To keep them focused on their studies was a great challenge for the best of

Sister Barbaralie with her baton

teachers. The last week of school I made a deal with the students: if you are attentive for the entire class, the final 15 minutes I will have some spectacular entertainment. This aroused their curiosity. One student asked, "Sister, are you going to do a strip-tease?"

The final week arrived. I was teaching Emerson and held their attention as I saw them glance periodically at the clock. "Sister, it's now time," one of the girls in the back of the room informed me. I went to the locker outside the room and took out my baton and CD player. I turned on "Stars and Stripes Forever" and began twirling. The students were mesmerized. All of a sudden, I felt a shift of energy in the room as I did the fingertip twirls. When I turned to do a figure eight, I saw Father D with his beady, brown eyes looking through the fire code window in the door. I was stunned, to say the least, but kept on twirling; even doing the body rolls and leg lifts. I have no idea how long he was peering at me. The students gave me a standing ovation.

Then, the mood shifted. I sensed a great love and concern for me from the students. "Sister, do you think Little Caesar is going to fire you?" they asked in all sincerity. "If he does, we will protest." Truthfully, I was asking the same question, but allayed their fears and said, "No, don't worry about me." I met Father D in the corridor later that day and he never said a word to me. The subject was never brought up. I hope he enjoyed my performance. However, years later another sister and I visited Father D at his retirement cottage. He jokingly asked me, "Did you bring your baton with you?"

My great joy is returning to St. Francis High School for reunions and special events. A school that was facing closure when I went there is one of the outstanding Catholic high schools in the country. It's rewarding to see the students I taught, now professional men and women, as loyal supporters and contributors to their "alma mater." The school has a Robinson Science Center, Kuhn Theatre, Kuhn Memorial Field, Kuhn Spyglass Fieldhouse, all possible through the donations of alumni, and even a "Barbaralie Stiefermann Library Fund."

As much as I loved St. Francis High School, I saw an opening for a campus minister at Northern Illinois University in DeKalb, Illinois and applied. Why not try something new? After several interviews, I was hired. My first morning there, after leaving my apartment across the street from the Newman Center, I was delayed by black men in turbans and colorful attire as they chanted and walked single file to the Student Center.

Father Don Ahles, Sister Barbaralie,
Father Bob Hoffman, director, Newman Center,
Northern Illinois University, 1981

What a spectacle to see—black men from another country. I had been accustomed to only Caucasian students in all previous assignments. I was excited! The whole world was my campus!

Campus ministry was quite a contrast to teaching. After the first two weeks, I felt as if I were "goofing off" and not doing any work. I was having too much fun. When I was sent to UCLA for training in campus ministry, one of the assignments given was going alone on the streets of Los Angeles at 9:00 a.m. and returning at 4:00 p.m., to share with the group how we ministered that day. After giving each of us a two-dollar bill, the instructor sent us on our way. The sharing was most interesting upon our return. Everyone's experiences were different. In fact, I was the only person who still had the two dollars. A gentleman paid for my lunch in a quaint, little restaurant as we conversed about T. S. Eliot. We ended our Eliot conversation talking about prayer. He felt uncomfortable with prayer, but "success in the spiritual quest required persistence," I said. In the words of T. S. Eliot, "'For us, there is only the trying. The rest is not our business.'"

This assignment and experience were symbolic to me of what campus ministry is all about. Precisely what Pope Francis is saying to the bishops and priests to leave their offices and go to the streets where the people are is "campus ministry."

I was hired as editor of *Newman Now* and Director of Spiritual Enrichment Programs. I had the good fortune to work with dynamic

Rite of Christian Initiation of Adults, Newman Center,
Sister Barbaralie, front middle, 1986

priests: Fathers Robert Hoffman, William McDonnell, and Daniel Hermes, as well as seven competent lay persons, including Colleen Metternick, Miss Congeniality and Miss Talent, in Miss America Pageant, 1973.

Every semester the Physical Education Department sponsored a panel consisting of all different lifestyles: married couple, gay couple, single, celibate, gay, lesbian, transgender, transvestite, etc. I represented the celibate lifestyle. The students came in droves for this event. I must admit I was nervous and apprehensive the first time I was asked to participate. What will the students ask me?

Sure enough. I was asked the first question: "Sister, as a Roman Catholic nun, how can you sit next to a homosexual, or even be on this panel?" Next question: "Sister, the Bible says, 'Be fruitful; multiply the earth.' How can you justify your lifestyle?" Third question: "I'm an atheist. I deeply admire you for the choice you've made. I could never live as a celibate. How can you live this life and be happy?" Question four: "Sister, you have all the plumbing. Why don't you use it?" Fifth question: "Did you ever wish you were married and have children?" Question six: "Do you like men?"

At one of the panels, Doctor Klink decided to try a different approach. Instead of introducing ourselves and our lifestyles, he had us remain anonymous and asked the audience for a show of hands. If the students knew the panel member, they were instructed not to vote. The questioning began, "How many think this woman is celibate? How many think she is married? How many think she is lesbian?" When these questions were asked, few students thought I was the celibate on stage. And finally, Doctor said, "Will the real celibate stand up; the real lesbian; the real married couple, etc." Needless to say, Doctor Klink attempted to show how we misjudge people. It was a learning lesson for all of us.

After 11 years of answering these and other questions, I became a pro on this panel. In fact, I felt as if I were on the Johnny Carson Show at times. Often great humor was injected and broke the tension for the entire panel. It always amazed me that I received more questions than any other member on the panel.

Many questions surfaced in my mind as a campus minister and other life experiences. The same questions John Shelby Spong, Episcopal bishop, asked were often my concerns: "Is celibacy the only moral alternative to marriage? Should the widowed be allowed to form intimate relationships without remarrying? Should the Church receive homosexuals into its community and support gay and lesbian relationships? Should congregations publicly and liturgically witness and affirm divorces? Should the Church's moral standards continue to be set by patriarchal males?"

I pose these questions in view of the changing realities of our times. And what should be the pastoral response to these realities? How does the church incorporate teaching about equal, loving, nonexploitative relationships?

One of the memorable trips I had with college students was to Austria. After traveling all night in the air and arriving by bus at our destination, the students insisted on going to a discotheque that evening. My reply was, "Did we come all the way to Austria to disco?"

When we arrived on the dance floor, all other students left and sat on the sides as we Americans discoed and they watched. I felt uneasy about the other students' withdrawal from the floor. I huddled our students together and told them to ask the ladies and gentlemen from the other countries to dance the next piece with them. The disc jockey did not think I would succeed in getting the other students to return to the floor. We later learned from the foreign students that they "felt inferior to the American students and would not compete with them."

Our mission was successful; all the other students returned to the dance floor with an American partner. It was gratifying to see them bonding, and even more thrilling, to hear the students from France request that each group perform a dance peculiar to their culture. What an education! France, Italy, Germany, Russia, Switzerland, Holland, were some of the countries that displayed their gifts of music and dance. The disc jockey scurried around in his repertoire for "Turkey in the Straw" for the American Square Dance.

At three in the morning, we decided to call it "quits," and I asked the disc jockey to play "It's a Small World," to which we all held hands in a circle and sang. The goodbyes, hugs, and tears captured the meaning of living in harmony with one another. I was tired, but happy I had allowed the students to go to the Austrian Discotheque, when my preference would have been a Viennese ballroom.

My eleven years' experiences as a campus minister could be an entire book. If my age weren't against me, I would be back on a college campus. At the end of my tenth year, another strong "call" brewed within me. I went to the La Casa Franciscan Renewal Center in Scottsdale, Arizona, for a meeting. After my time there with other School Sisters of St. Francis and Associates, I remained several days in the desert to pray. While in the mountains, the resurgence to write came with every sunrise and sunset.

When I returned to Northern Illinois University, I thought the college scene would shatter this inner call. Such was not the case. Rilke's *Letters to a Young Poet* began to speak loudly and cleverly to me:

> Nobody can counsel and help you, nobody. There is only one single way. Go into yourself. Search for the reason that bids you to write; find out whether it is spreading out its roots in the deepest places of your heart, acknowledge to yourself whether you would have to die if it were denied you to write. This above all—ask yourself in the stillest hour of your night: Must I write? Delve into yourself for a deep answer.
> . . . . . .

After searching in the stillness of night, I realized I must respond to the call. I finally wrote to Sister Frances Cunningham, President of the School Sisters of St. Francis, and told her of my desert experience. Sister, intrigued with the aspect of "call," asked me to send samples of my writings and she gave her blessing to the writing of *Stanislaus...with feet in the world.* This is a biography of a ten-year old orphan girl who was entrusted to the foundresses of our order in 1874. Eventually, Theresa Hegner became Sister Stanislaus, and then Mother General of the School Sisters of St. Francis. The history that unfolds in this book is not only one of dates and

Autograph Party, 1990
Sisters Marietta Hanus and Barbaralie

places, but rather a history of people and movements. The librarian at the University of Chicago said, "Of its genre, *Stanislaus* is the best book on our shelves."

(It was during this time my mother was ill and died. Because of the profound experience of her dying, I have devoted Chapter XI to her death in order to share with you, the reader, that death can be beautiful.)

After I completed writing the book, I held an interim job in the community while waiting for it to be published. As Associate Relationship Director, I had an office in Milwaukee, and an office in Omaha, Nebraska, for Tau Volunteers.

Previously, I had made friends with people in Omaha when I taught Tai Chi in a Summer Enrichment Program there. One of these friends was Sharon Coyle, who called me in the Tau Volunteer office one afternoon and said, "Barbaralie, we are going on a firewalk tomorrow afternoon." I can still hear the excitement in her voice when she said, "And you've got to go with me." I immediately responded, "Sharon, you're going on the firewalk, not I."

"I already paid your $75; you must go," she said.

"Oh well, I will go with you," I said, "but I'm not going on the firewalk."

We drove for miles in the late afternoon through a rural area outside of Omaha and came to a farm with a huge barn. As we drove up and parked the car, we saw many other participants make their way into the barn to be seated. The instructor, who was from Norway, had great experience in conducting firewalks around the world. She began by asking the question, "Why did you come here?" to which 43 participants individually said their names aloud and responded. A gentleman from Iowa said, "I am 65 years old and all my life I've been motivated by fear. I just want to rid myself of all this fear." Another person said, "I'm 40 years old this week and I wanted to do something exciting for my birthday." I responded by giving my name but not identifying myself as sister, and said, "I'm here because my friend insisted I come." I no more than completed the sentence and one of the participants loudly proclaimed, "Oh, Sister Barbaralie, I heard you give a speech in Montreal!"

I couldn't believe it. I'm on a remote farm in Nebraska far away from home, and somebody was able to identify me. I had given Sharon strict orders that I wanted no one to know I'm a sister. Now everyone knew I was Sister Barbaralie!

For six consecutive summers, I had attended an international conference sponsored by the International Institute of Integral Human

Sciences in Montreal, Canada. I owe a great debt of gratitude to Doctors Marilyn and John Rossner, chairpersons of the conference for literally exposing me to a whole new world. Speakers included world religious leaders, United Nations representatives, astronauts, healers, psychics, mediums, mystics, UFO contactees and experts, medical doctors, musicians, dramatists, educators for peace.

Sister Barbaralie after perfoming the Chinese Ribbon Dance in Montreal, Canada, 1988

The conference in 1989 was entitled "Cosmic Vision … for a New World." In particular, I remember Sri Swami Satchidananda's presentation: "Cosmic Consciousness for a New World Order in the Global Village." Apollo Astronaut Dr. Brian O'Leary spoke on "Cosmic Quest: The Mars Project and the Search for Extra-Terrestrial Intelligence and UFO's." A presentation given by a Brazilian Spiritista medium, Divaldo Franco, entitled: "The Cosmic Revelations of the Spirit World" was fascinating, as was Dr. Otho Wingo's insights from Polynesian Huna: "Our Multiple Selves and Cosmic Vision." It was at this specific conference that I spoke about "The Cosmic Vision of St. Francis Assisi: Its Implications for Today." I learned that people from all over the world loved St. Francis.

In 1988, I was also a guest speaker: "Developing a Cosmic Spirituality for Personal and Social Transformation." I remember some of my opening remarks: If we are going to speak about cosmic energy, cosmic power, cosmic destruction, then we need to seriously reflect upon a cosmic spirituality. As human beings we cannot deal with cosmic energy and our responsibility for it without a cosmic spirituality.

I later asked the participant at the firewalk which conference she had attended. I was amazed at her answer. "I think it was 1988. You quoted Otto Rank, the Austrian psychoanalyst, 'When religion lost the cosmos, society became neurotic and had to invent psychology to deal with the neurosis.' And I'm a psychologist," she said with a laugh.

By this time our firewalk instructor called us into the barn again after each of us had carried an armful of wood to a place, distant from the building, to build a bonfire. Now her question to each of us was: "What are your fears in walking over hot coals?" The fears were as varied as the number of participants. "I'm afraid of landing in a hospital with third-degree burns on my feet," I said aloud. What I did not say audibly, was I feared my provincial would question how I burned my feet. I was also concerned about hospital costs and debilitating effects for life.

After spending time processing "fear," we again proceeded outdoors to add more wood to the pile to be burned. Then we came back inside and talked about the symbols of fire, particularly in the Old Testament. Back and forth we went between getting primed to do this courageous and treacherous act, to building the wood pile, which ended up being higher than the barn. All the while I'm thinking: Do I really want to do this? Instead of allaying my fears, I felt I was creating more fears in my life.

Eventually, the instructor handed a black woman a gallon of kerosene and told her to walk around the woodpile and pour until the container was empty. Then there was another ritual lighting the fire. Holy smokes! The fire devoured the wood furiously and fast. Flames shot up into the sky like a rocket taking off.

As the fire blazed in the darkness, we went back inside the barn to be given final instructions. There was to be absolute silence standing around the simmering coals. No one was to force anyone to walk across the bed of coals. It was our choice and when we felt ready. This must be done with bare feet. After walking across 15 to 20 feet of hot coals, there was a patch of mud to soothe the feet. "Do not run, but walk with a steady, determined gait. Hold up your right arm as you charge forth and say aloud "cold moss; cold moss."

The time had come. All gathered in a circle around the coals smoldering in their final stages. I ran quickly and hid behind a nearby tree to remove my pantyhose. After all, I did not plan to do the firewalk. I entered the circle. The first person to begin the firewalk was the man from Iowa. He charged across, and I could tell when he arrived on the patch of soothing mud, he felt he had overcome a big fear. His smile proclaimed victory. One by one, people walked across. I waited. I saw Sharon successfully reach the mud. I waited until several more people went and marveled that no one's feet seemed to burn as they walked.

My mother had died about a month before, so I pictured her at the end of the walk with outstretched arms waiting to greet me. I charged across and Mom was there to give me a big hug. My feet never felt so good as I walked in the cool, soothing mud.

Only one person lost her focus and jumped off the hot coals before finishing. I believe that after six hours of priming us to engage in such an activity, we walked across hot coals in our ethereal body rather than the physical. It was an experience I cannot convey in words. Am I happy I went on the firewalk? Yes!

Sharon and I were on a "high" as we drove through miles of country in the dark and had no idea where we were going and how to get back home and truthfully, didn't care. We finally saw a roadside inn and stopped. The gentleman gave vague directions in how to get to Omaha. We then called some of our sisters in Tucson at two in the morning and told them of our experience. They were awakened suddenly and declared us "loony," as they laughed and went back to sleep.

After the publication of my book, I chose to teach at Chaparral College, a career college in Tucson, Arizona. I loved the mountain

Sister Barbaralie, Chaparral College, Tucson, Arizona English, Oral Communication, Personal Development, 1992

ranges, beautiful sunsets, and diversity of people I taught. I became career oriented as I walked down a corridor at the college and saw myself in a full-length mirror with the caption above "Are you dressed for success?" Another corridor reminded students of their posture: "Look at yourself; do you convey confidence?"

I taught English, Oral Communication and Personal Development to Hispanics, Native Americans, Mexicans, Caucasians and Blacks. At times I questioned who was teaching who. I learned as much from them as they learned from me, especially when they wrote of their experiences.

I won't forget Melanie, a young mother, who read her composition to the class and described in detail how she became a gang member. I tried not to show any reaction when she said, "I was required to do three drive-by shootings and succeeded." She also went on to say how the gang members were her greatest community and support, and were very protective of her four-year old son. I held back tears when she ended her writing with the words, "Every night before I leave my apartment to go into the unknown, I pray: Dear God, protect me as I walk into the darkness. You are a loving God who created me and loves me with all my faults and failings. Surround me with your light and love this night. In your embrace, whom or what should I fear? O God, you are my defense and security. In your love is my sole safety: of whom shall I be afraid?"

There were so many times I had the urge to teach religion instead of English and Oral Communication. At times I found it difficult not to impose my moral standards upon these students. In my own subtle way, I tried to be their compass and guide them in another direction.

Melanie was an A student. Isn't it a sad commentary on society that young men and women find their greatest support and community in belonging to a gang? I encountered many students searching and trying to find their way in life. I am convinced that the search for self and the quest for God are one and the same.

As a Franciscan, I gained a greater appreciation of all Creation from Native Americans. To watch a Hopi Indian woman ask permission of Mother Earth to take some of her soil and to remove only what she needed to make a bowl is a lesson for all of us in our culture so prone to greed. Then to watch her mold and shape the bowl was meditation for her and me. To observe a Navajo Indian woman weave a blanket as she silently meditated with every stitch and vibrant color moved me to an inner space of wonder and contemplation.

The Native Americans are people of stillness and silence. When I taught them, I felt they listened to my thoughts. The Native people perceived themselves to be an integral part of Creation. Their writings and speeches amused me, especially when they spoke of Creation in family terms: Mother Earth, Grandmother Moon, Grandfather Winds. This is also reminiscent of St. Francis of Assisi when he spoke of Brother Sun and Sister Moon. Chief Seattle said:

> The earth does not belong to people; people belong to the earth…
> This earth is precious to the Creator and to harm the earth is to heap
> contempt upon its Creator… Our dead never forget this beautiful earth,

for it is the mother of the red people. We are part of the earth and it is part of us.

It was difficult to think of leaving the mountains, the sunshine, and diversity of Tucson to move to another location. My dad was 99 years old in St. Joseph Home, conducted by the Carmelite Sisters in Jefferson City, Missouri. The thought of being in Tucson where I could not be with him more often bothered me. I finally decided after five years at Chaparral College to move to St. Louis.

My sister Betty, her husband John Posgay, and their daughter Laura rented and furnished an apartment for me on South Kingshighway Boulevard in St. Louis. The beautiful and spacious apartments were originally built for army officers and their wives. After I moved, I worked at Crown Medical Equipment Company, owned by the Posgays. This job was totally out of my element since I was an educator, but I was able to transfer many skills and enjoy different work while I pursued other ministries in St. Louis. The medical field was tough, complicated and involved lots of paper work. I learned a great deal during those eight months.

Having been away from music for 25 years, Sue Brown, principal of St. Raphael Archangel School in St. Louis, hired me in 1997. The dignified pastor, Monsignor William A. Drennan, questioned Sue's decision in hiring someone who had taught on the college level and having to adjust to elementary school, especially having been away from music for many years. The two of them often joked about it later. Sue was happy she had proved Monsignor Drennan wrong. Sue Brown is now the Director of Marketing and Community Relations in the archdiocese.

What did I teach at St. Raphael's that made a lasting impression on me, and hopefully, the students? With the support of Sue and the faculty, I put on a Christmas musical each year with the entire school. My first musical was "*Something's Up Down in Bethlehem.*" It was a great success. Parents and students loved it! The next year we performed "*Christmas Around the World.*" Mary Cauley, a former dance teacher who taught art in the school, assisted in teaching the choreography. What a pleasure it was teaching these students and seeing the joy on their faces after a spectacular performance.

Not only did we do musicals, but I introduced liturgical dance in this affluent, conservative parish. I challenged the eighth grade girls and parishioners to respond to the invitation "to praise God's name in the festive dance (Ps 149:3)." The power and beauty of dance is a human form of prayer, praise and worship. I explained to the girls that in Western civilization we think of dance for entertainment or courtship rather than in a religious context. Yet we have a wonderful tradition of "folk" dance in Western culture in which people join together to express their joy and the beauty of human community.

A good example of such a "dance of the folk" was on the Copacabana Beach in Rio de Janeiro where millions of people, including bishops and priests, joined in a simple but lively dance at the closing liturgy with Pope Francis on World Youth Day in July, 2013. I was elated when I saw it on television and wished I had been there.

A parishioner made beautiful, white choral gowns with blue satin stoles for the girls. After numerous practices in the church's large sanctuary, they anxiously awaited to offer their gift of dance at the opening Sunday Mass for Catholic Education Week. I was proud of them as they gracefully and reverently conveyed the beauty of the human body in worship and prayer. Monsignor Drennan, associate pastor, Father Matthew O'Toole, Sue Brown, parishioners and students sat in awe. The eighth-grade girls' self-esteem rose to new heights as they asked, "Sister, may we do it again real soon?" And we did.

While I was at St. Raphael the Archangel School, two important events in my personal life happened. I celebrated my Golden Jubilee as a School Sister of St. Francis. The school personnel ignored my wishes and went all out for this celebration in May, 2000. Miss Noeleen Hannigan, a native of Ireland and eighth grade teacher, must have planned months in advance for this occasion. I received congratulatory messages from Missouri State senators and representatives. Clarence Harmon, mayor of St. Louis declared "Sister Barbaralie Day," May 22, 2000. Archbishop Justin Rigali sent a beautiful congratulatory letter, as did other dignitaries, people, and parishioners in St. Louis.

The day began with a procession from the school to the church with faculty and students. Monsignor Drennan and Father O'Toole celebrated Mass, as Sue Brown played the organ and the children sang. I renewed my vows publicly at which members of my family in St. Louis were also present. After Mass, dinner was served to the priests, Sue Brown, and my family. When we had finished eating, we went to school where the eighth grade class put on a skit for the entire school.

The spoof on me exhibited theatrical talent of these budding students. In addition, each class did a booklet of appreciation. My sister-in-law, Mary and brother Charles who were at St. Raphael's for the celebration, had another one for me in Frankenstein at Our Lady, Help of Christians Parish in October, 2000. Since my roots are in Frankenstein, the Golden Jubilee was special there.

My religious community has an annual celebration near June 13th, the day of our reception. The year 2000 was no exception. To be with my classmates as well as 25, 60, 70, 75, and 80 year jubilarians is a powerful manifestation of dedicated services and commitment of women religious. The blessings of community life filled my heart with deep gratitude that day.

The other event in my life was the death of my father on May 14, 1997, at age 100 and four months. I went to visit Daddy in Jefferson City on Ascension Thursday, which used to be a day off in a Catholic school. We had lunch together at St. Joseph Home and enjoyed what was to be our last visit. He told me he had had a strange feeling in his throat, but that it had gone and he felt fine. The next morning, I received a call from my sister Theresa that Daddy had a stroke and was no longer able to speak and swallow. All the family gathered around him on his five final days on earth.

Daddy in his mid 90s
Photo courtesy: Siobhan O'Brien

I was grateful I had moved from Tucson. I was the last member of the family that Daddy spoke to before his stroke. To hear him say, "You are beautiful," still echoes in my heart.

What a privilege and sacred act it was to be present with Daddy in his dying. He drew his last breath when his only son, Charles, was with him. His five daughters went to have dinner with Mary, our sister-in-law. How appropriate that Daddy chose to die with Charles. For the four years he was in St. Joseph Home, Charles attended daily Mass with him before going to work.

Death was not the opposite of life for my beloved father. As Christians, we believe the opposite of death is birth. Life is eternal. I drew strength from Echart Tolle:

> When you sit with a dying person, do not deny any aspect of that experience. Do not deny what is happening and do not deny your feelings. The recognition that there is nothing you can do may make you feel helpless, sad, or angry. Accept what you feel. Then go one step further: accept that there is nothing you can do, and accept it completely. You are not in control. Deeply surrender to every aspect of that experience, your feelings as well as any pain or discomfort the dying person may be experiencing. Your surrendered state of consciousness and the stillness that comes with it will greatly assist the dying person and ease their transition. If words are called for, they will come out of the stillness within you. But they will be secondary. With the stillness comes the benediction: peace.

Stiefermann Family, mid 1980s
Back: Daddy, Theresa, Barbaralie
Middle: Mom, Charles, Betty
Front: Kathleen, Margaret

After five years of being near family and teaching at St. Raphael School, the United States provincials summoned me back to Milwaukee in 2001 to be the Director of Alfons Art Gallery and Gift Shop. This came as a great surprise to me. I never thought or dreamed of being in an art gallery even though I love and appreciate good art. My sister Betty specialized in oil painting and won awards for her art pieces. As family, we often visited art museums and went to art fairs and festivals. Mom enjoyed going to the Chicago Art Institute to see her favorite paintings when visiting my sister Margaret.

It is rare that a religious community can pride itself in having its own art gallery. The School Sisters of St. Francis have a rich heritage in art. One of our early artists was Sister Elizabeth Fichtner, born in Baden, Germany, who came to America in 1895 and entered the community in

1905. She, as well as two other great artists, Sisters Berchmans Schmidt and Johanna Endres were sent to Munich, Germany, to study at the Alte Pinakothek from 1909-1912. I found it interesting that they were handed three sticks of color paint: red, blue, and yellow and were told to find a painting they liked and copy it. On their return to the United States, they attended classes at the Chicago Art Institute and Milwaukee art schools where they received the same instruction as in Munich. Their instructor was the well-known American artist, Carl Maar.

"Wood Gatherer" by Jules Bastien-LePage; oil on canvas copy by Sister Elizabeth Fichtner

Sister Elizabeth was famous as a copy artist of the old masters, which was an acceptable art form at that time. When I entered the convent, 21 of her large paintings hung in the art parlors, which later became Alfons Gallery, named after co-foundress Mother Alfons, who had loved and promoted art and music. Sister Elizabeth's copy of the "Wood Gatherer" by Jules Bastien-LePage was and is one of my favorites. The original painting is in the Milwaukee Art Museum.

My predecessor, who began the gallery in 1991, Sister Lucinda Hubing, exhibited internationally with the Smithsonian travel exhibits,

Sister Lucinda Hubing doing cloisonné

and nationally and locally won 45 awards. She received her Master of Fine Arts from Notre Dame University with further study at the Cleveland Art Institute under Kenneth Bates, who is considered the "Father of Enameling" in the United States. She studied sculpture with Mestrovic and fresco painting with Jean Charlot. Because of the amount and quality of the artwork she accomplished, the National Museum of Women Artists in Washington, D. C., asked for slides of her work to open a scholar's file in her name. She conducted tours abroad yearly between 1969 and 1994 to fifty-two countries, visiting their leading museums.

Now, how would you like to follow in Sister Lucinda's footsteps in being the director of Alfons Gallery? That's what I had to do. I learned later that she, along with Sister Phyllis Vater, vice-president of the international congregation, were the ones who suggested I become the director.

Fortunately, Sister Lucinda mentored me for several months since I had had no formal training in art; I was piped full of music! Every six to eight weeks, I installed a new exhibit. Alfons Gallery was a sought-after venue by local artists and art groups. The four lay volunteers who worked with Sister Lucinda continued under my leadership.

After many years of hammering nails into walls, the gallery showed signs of use and abuse. In 2004, I had the gallery remodeled from ceiling to floor and installed the Walker System for exhibiting paintings. To this day, under the leadership of Valerie Christell, Alfons Gallery is thriving in an economy that forced many other galleries to close.

I also learned much from Sister Helena Steffensmeier, whose art graces our entire building and other institutions of the School Sisters of St. Francis. She made use of many different media: wood, fiber, oil, clay, marble, metal, alabaster, bronze, acrylics and watercolor. She created forms that revealed the spirit which animated her life as a religious and educator. This spirit expressed itself in artworks that suggest the immediacy and dramatic sincerity of the

Sister Helena Steffensmeier

primitive styles Sister Helena admired.

Recipient of many awards, Sister Helena also had national art exhibits. She was featured on CBS "Sunday Morning with Charles Kuralt;" "Heart of the Nation," and "Real to Reel." Her work was featured in publications: *Designing and Stitching and Applique, Textile Art in the Church, Seasons of Friendship*. Her artwork was pictured in magazines: *Anno Domini, U.S. Catholic, Christian Art* and others.

Sister Helena believed that "art is the most intimate expression of one's intimate life." Her work expresses tenderness toward humankind, strength and joy in facing demands of creative work, boundless spontaneity and dignity.

How fortunate I was to be friends of our many sister artists, most of whom are now enjoying eternal life. These sisters enriched my life immensely. It is through the arts that we experience mysticism, vision, and conversion. Art invites us to imagine new things, expand our wealth of ideas for dealing with what life presents to us, offers connections to all facets of creation.

My life has been enhanced by members of the Fine Arts Society and the Milwaukee Art Museum. The lectures, outings, socials and friendships are all part of the mosaic that is me. The Art Museum with its beautiful Calatrava wing on Lake Michigan is a wonder to behold. It's gratifying to see the many visitors who come there to feed their souls.

After eleven years as director of Alfons Gallery, I retired at age 80. As I reflect on those years, I am deeply grateful that every day I went to work, I was surrounded by beauty and the creative energy of all the artists, both living and dead, who fashioned those works of art. How many people can say that about their jobs?

Isn't it unfortunate that people in general do not look upon artists as workers. When I was a campus minister, I heard parents say to their son or daughter, "get a real job." Sad to say, many talented artists are having to forfeit their talents in artistry because they cannot make a living expressing the beauty of God through ballet, painting, carving, music, etc. What a deprived people we become when we indulge only in business, technology and science. I feel strongly that when we are deprived of the power of expression, we will express ourselves in a drive for unharnessed and destructive power. It is through our creative powers, through the imagination, that peace will ultimately be achieved.

Chapter IX
Tearing Down the Wall of Prejudice

Donald was a precocious child when I taught him in first grade at St. Irene School. In fact, I could single him out on the first day of school as a bright, creative, and spontaneous child. As young as he was, he became my little helper. I read aloud a story called "The Little Red

Donald Jansen, 7th grade

Fox." He listened intently and then raised his hand and waved it until I called on him. "May we dramatize this story?" he asked with great excitement. Within minutes, he organized the students, who volunteered to play a role. It was then that I not only saw his dramatic flair, but his leadership skills in dealing with people.

After five years of teaching first grade, I was assigned sixth grade, the following year seventh, followed by eighth. Thus, Donald and his classmates had me as their teacher for four of their elementary school years. As a teacher, it was a great study to have the same children for this length of time. The class was unusual. For the most part, the students were intelligent, highly motivated and goal oriented. Teaching them was sheer delight.

When they were in sixth grade, the classroom became hot, so hot that when Donald put his hand on the wall, he said, "Sister, there's something wrong! May I go down to the boiler room and see what's going on?" I would entrust only Donald with such a mission and gave my permission. Before he returned to my class, he ran to the eighth grade room and told Sister Adria, the principal, to call Bollweg's Heating and Cooling Company. He frantically told her the boiler is ready to explode. She, too, had wondered about the excessive heat.

Mr. Bollweg's business was located near the school. Within a matter of minutes, he was in the basement checking the boiler. Sure enough, Donald was right. Mr. Bollweg, who had several of his own children in the school said, "Within twenty more minutes, this boiler would have exploded and blown up the entire school."

I thanked Donald for saving our lives and the school by giving him a Hershey bar that I had in my desk. I learned later from another student that Donald gave the candy bar to a child in fifth grade who had a cleft palate and was often ostracized in games during recess.

I relied on Donald during science classes in seventh and eighth grades to help with the experiments. One of the projects in the science book was installing a door bell. I thought I followed the instructions meticulously, but in the final step, the doorbell never rang. Donald raised his hand and said, "Sister, I think I know what went wrong." He proceeded to the front of the room, took apart some of what I had done, redid it, and presto! The doorbell rang and the students applauded Donald.

Another science project was building a small airplane. Before beginning the project, I assigned Donald to be in charge and work with several other students at home. When they completed the assignment, they were to bring the plane to school and we would test its flight outdoors. Within a week, the students brought the plane to school as we all gathered outside. The students clapped and clapped as the plane took off into the sky and finally landed in a neighbor's yard. It was as great an achievement to the students as the Wright Brothers' first flight was to my dad who had witnessed that flight many, many years ago.

Not to show partiality to Donald was difficult. He read the Bible from cover to cover when he was in seventh grade. In geography class one afternoon, I called on Donald to answer a question. It was unusual for him not to have a clue what I had asked, so he fumbled and rumbled, trying to give an answer. I slowly walked down the aisle to his desk. There in front of his large geography book that he held upright was his Bible opened as he was reading "Daniel's Vision of a Ram and Goat." I reprimanded him as he blushed and said, "I'm sorry."

When Father Stier gave religious instructions to the eighth graders, he quoted a Scripture passage from Mark's gospel of the "Parable of the Mustard Seed." Father gave a wrong reference to the parable. Donald politely said, "Father, I think you mean Mark 4:30." I will never forget the look on the pastor's face. He was shocked that Donald was able to cite the reference without any previous study or preparation. I later told Father, "This is the challenge I face every day."

The pastor invariably called on Donald to serve Mass for special events. He was an incredible young master of ceremonies for all religious functions, especially during Holy Week services. Sometimes I wanted him to sing on the choir because he was also an alert and good singer, but usually the pastor succeeded in getting him at the altar.

Donald graduated from St. Irene's with honors and attended St. Francis High School. In spite of his high school activities, Donald still stayed connected to the parish. Periodically, he would come to the convent and relate to me what and how he was doing in high school. I always enjoyed visiting with him, and at times, he assisted in my classroom when I made preparations for a new school year.

Donald graduated with honors from St. Francis High School and enrolled in St. Procopius College, run by the Benedictine priests in Lisle, Illinois. He liked it there and began to discern his own call of becoming a priest. I rarely saw Donald during his college years, but periodically, I received a phone call from him. I distinctly remember one of the calls where he stated to me, "I feel as if I'm going to die young, but don't feel sad. Know that I have lived a full life."

I lived in an apartment near Chicago's Lincoln Park during the summer I was studying for orals in English for my master's degree at Loyola University. Friends of mine, Paul and Maryan Panucci, lived in this apartment but were in Italy for the entire summer and asked if I would live in their dwelling while they were away. I was happy to be alone to study for orals and near Loyola. Also, when attending the Berlitz School of Foreign Languages and pursuing doctoral studies— spending hours in the Newberry and Chicago Public Libraries—I spent nights and occasional weekends with the Panucci's. I enjoyed not only their company, but Italian cuisine at their home and at the renown Italian Village restaurant in downtown Chicago.

One night as I was reviewing my notes in Milton's *Paradise Lost*, the telephone rang. I was startled by the ring, for I had told no one of my whereabouts except the sisters at St. Irene's. To my great surprise, Donald was on the phone. He said he had gotten the number from the sisters. Then he said, "If you aren't too busy tonight, may I come over to see you?"

"Yes, I would be happy to see you," was my immediate response.

About one half hour later, in walks Donald with a bottle of wine and Lay's chips. I gave him a big hug all the while wondering what this visit was about. My silent questioning was answered shortly after Donald arrived. As we sat sipping Cabernet Sauvignon, Donald cautiously said,

"Sister, I have always loved you more than any other teacher I've had, and I know you loved me as your student." I listened intently as he continued, "I have something to say to you tonight, and I hope you are going to still love me."

"Donald, no matter what you say to me tonight, I will always love you," I said. "Sister, I am gay," he said. What a shock to me! I grasped for words. "Donald, I still love you, but if you are coming for help, I am the person least qualified to counsel you. As a matter of fact, I must confess, I am prejudiced against homosexuals. The Catholic Church's teachings and the Scriptures have instilled my prejudice," I said. Donald could see I was stunned. The student I loved was gay. "Now that I have knowledge of your sexual orientation, should that alter my love for you?" I asked.

I sat silently drinking my wine and reached for some chips.

"Sister, you have taught me many things over the years. Now let me teach you about homosexuality," he said. "There is a gay bar on Belmont Street, not too far from here. I want to introduce you to our life style. Won't you go with me tonight to the bar?" he pleadingly asked.

We were still in a modified habit, so I said, "I surely don't want to be recognized as a sister, so I'll check out Maryan's clothes. Since she was a former performer and singer, I'm sure she has something I can wear," I said as I excused myself and went into her bedroom. I had many beautiful selections from which to choose. I chose a long-sleeved, royal blue silk dress with sequins around the V-neckline. The dress was beautiful on me. Even Donald smiled as he said, "You look stunning."

As we walked out the door, I said, "Donald, am I safe in going out at this hour of the night?" "You are very safe, I assure you nothing will happen to you," Donald emphatically stated. I could not have had a better escort. Donald was always a gentleman, and now, even more so, as he opened and closed the car door on the passenger side for me. As a woman, it is always a pleasure for me to experience these common courtesies.

We entered the dimly lit bar and sat at a table in the corner. Donald ordered wine for the two of us. I sat in silence watching men embracing and kissing one another. Not once did any man even look at me. Few women were in the bar. It all seemed strange to me. The words of Scripture flashed through my mind. St. Paul wrote:

Their women exchanged natural relations for unnatural, and the men likewise gave up natural relations with women and were consumed with passion for one another, men committing shameless acts with men and receiving in their person the due penalty for their error. (Rm. 1:26-27).

In this passage, Paul is certainly bringing out the evilness of homosexuality. And what about the Holiness Codes in the book of Leviticus? I asked myself. Homosexuality is condemned, but so are many other practices: child sacrifice, using mediums or sorcerers, incest, intercourse during menstruation, and bestiality.

Leviticus does not specifically state the nature of the homosexual liaison as being forbidden. Was this an invasive act, an imposition of the stronger man upon a weaker man? And was there mutuality? Death was the penalty inflicted on both persons, thus implying an act of mutual consent, but in the cases of bestiality, the code also calls for death of both man and animal. How could an animal be a consenting participant?

I felt as if my thoughts on homosexuality were all tangled up as Donald sat in front of me. As I continued to observe the behavior in the bar, Donald pointed out some of the gentlemen: the president of a bank who was also married to a woman, the CEO of a company, gay but also married with children. And, of course, gay, single, men in love with one another. I realized more and more the little knowledge I had on homosexuality was shaped by the Scriptures and the interpretations given by so-called scholars. I, myself, at one time, had written an article in the *Warrenville Digest* condemning homosexuals and their behavior. I'm sure Donald read that article since he lived in town. I was afraid to ask. I questioned my upbringing. I did not learn this prejudice from my parents. That topic was never brought up in our family in my formative years.

Donald and I went back to the apartment and continued the conversation. He told me that his family disowned him; he was literally told to get out of the house and never to return. These were good, Catholic parents subject to the same teaching as I. He also related to me how he struggled to identify his sexual orientation by living with a young lady for a year, thinking he was bisexual. He also had a strong calling to the priesthood, but when he shared this with a priest, he was told he may not become a priest because he was homosexual.

Since Donald had been ousted from his parents' home at a young age, I asked him how he survived. "I went to live in Chicago," he said. "I was desperate for a job, so I saw a sign at Lyon & Healy's for someone to demonstrate organs. I applied and was hired," he said with a smile. I immediately said, "But you've never had organ lessons, how did you manage that?" "I used to watch you play the organ and learned by observation. And it may interest you to know, that for an entire year, I rebuilt an old pipe organ in one of the Episcopal churches in Chicago. And it sounded fantastic when I finished!" he said with a smile.

I was dumbfounded listening to this young man's struggles. It seemed incomprehensible to me that Donald, who was intelligent, talented, loving, kind, and handsome should ever have experienced so many hurdles in his young life. He was also a deeply spiritual and religious person who, as he said, "prayed non-stop to God to help and guide him on the right path."

I gave Donald a big embrace that night, and with tears streaming down my face, said, "Thank you for opening my eyes, ears and heart tonight, Donald. I will put the Bible aside for now, since it is not a resource in making decisions about issues of sexual ethics. I will read anything I can get my hands on to understand homosexuality. I want to learn more; tonight was only the beginning," I said as I held his hand tightly.

Donald looked at me in a way that only love can convey. For just a moment in his exile, the vision of inclusiveness was imagined. In that moment, the God of Creation spoke and declared to him and me, "I have looked out on everything I have made and behold it is very good" (Gen. 1:31).

Donald left my apartment with a happy heart that night whereas, my heart was heavy. I realized I had much homework to do. I regretted that I had spent so many of my youthful years bearing a prejudice that did not allow me to live in God's presence as a bearer of God's image. The beauty and wonder of the God of Creation was shrunken by the limits of my vision and small-minded thinking. The Judeo-Christian West had its strong tentacles in me, and after meeting Donald, I knew I had to tear down this wall of prejudice.

I diligently chiseled away at it. I learned through reading that neither Islam nor Hinduism sees homosexual activity as taboo. Primitive peoples like the Eskimos, Malaysians, and North American Indians had no difficulty in accepting it. I was amazed when I learned that ancient Greece institutionalized it. As a matter of fact, in some primitive cultures, a homosexual was seen as a kind of shaman or holy man, certainly not as a criminal worthy of death as viewed in the Bible. Once I gained knowledge and understanding of homosexuals, my love never wavered for the many people in our society who have been so ostracized, rejected and even hated.

Donald kept in touch with me, primarily by telephone. At times our conversations were quite lengthy. On one occasion, he thanked me for being a mother to him. He must have had a premonition regarding death at an early age. Once more he said to me, "I feel I will die as a young man, but I know I have experienced more than any sixty-year old man, so don't cry when I die. I am grateful that I have lived a full life."

That was the last call I received from Donald. Long were the days of inevitable waiting on my part; I suspected something was wrong. One late afternoon, I received a call, but it was not from Donald. A classmate of his informed me that Donald died of pancreatitis on the street in Chicago. The police searched for an identity and could find none on his person. Consequently, they placed him in the County Morgue hoping that sooner or later, someone would identify him.

Donald had an uncle who was a Chicago policeman. His uncle was searching for another body at the County Morgue when to his dismay, he spotted his nephew Donald. The uncle was shocked, to say the least, and informed the parents of the sad news.

Donald had a large funeral in St. Irene Church at which many of his classmates were present. I tried to heed his advice "not to cry," but as I reflected on his journey of 28 years, I allowed the tears to flow gently. How could I refrain from crying at the loss of someone who touched my life significantly. I stood by his parents at the grave site and observed his mother standing like a marble statue. She turned to me and said, "I know my son has gone to hell." I touched her gently and said as I looked into her eyes, "I proclaim your son, Saint Donald."

I was teaching at St. Francis High School at this time. For days after Donald's funeral, I had such a feeling of emptiness, nothingness, the zero point. I realized more than ever that growth in the human person takes place in the dark underground. There, where "no image has ever reached into the soul's foundation," as Meister Eckhart said, "God alone works."

It is amazing how Donald, unknowingly, prepared me for what was yet to come in my own life. When I went to UCLA for orientation in campus ministry, I was assigned a project with two students who happened to be gay. What a pleasure it was to work with these talented, young men. I was grateful I had torn down the wall of prejudice and could accept these gentlemen for who they were. I enjoyed every moment with them. "I am a part and parcel of the whole, and I cannot find God apart from the rest of humanity," Gandhi explicitly stated. When I left Los Angeles, it was Gary and Jim who drove me to the airport and sent me off with red roses.

When I arrived back at Northern Illinois University, among my many other tasks, I was asked to minister to the gay community. After my experiences with Donald, I welcomed the opportunity and felt that he had a hand in arranging this. There were many sad times and glad times with them. Dying of AIDS was quite prevalent then. Many students did not want their parents to be notified. Other students had been rejected by family and removed from the home. I told an Italian student, who sought my advice as to whether or not to inform his parents, not to do so. He felt he was keeping something from them and chose to tell them. Late at night, there was a knock on my door, and just as I had warned, he was thrown out of the house and ended up sleeping on my sofa.

I have seen the pain, the suicidal attempts, the fears and anxieties of homosexuals. I am happy that at this time there is much more openness and tolerance of them in the Church and society. I am grateful that the harsh, often unenlightened attitudes and practices that have long characterized a pastoral approach have diminished. Homosexuals are human beings in need of the same love and understanding as heterosexuals.

Some of my closest and most loyal friends are gay. When I opened myself to them, they were able to touch me. They loved me and shared with me the integrity and life-giving power present in their relationships. Where there is sincere affection, responsibility, and an authentic human relationship—where there is true love—God is surely present.

Chapter X

The Love Story

When I was sent to teach at St. Irene School in Warrenville, I had not yet completed my college degree. Consequently, I spent my summers at Alverno College in Milwaukee pursuing my degree. This was not only a time for academic growth but an opportunity to be with several other orders of sisters who attended Alverno. At that time, lay women, contrary to the present, were in the minority.

The summer of 1958, while studying at Alverno, I had a strange dream. Normally, I do not remember my dreams. In fact, the five dreams I do remember in my lifetime, were prophetic and came true, each involving tragedy and sad happenings. For this reason, I'm sure I repress my dreams to this day.

This particular dream was a puzzle to me. I saw a priest in a black suit and Roman collar getting off a ship. He was stately in his demeanor, blue eyes, handsome, with beautiful wavy, white hair, and a gentle smile. He spoke to me in a foreign language, which I did not understand. All other passengers that I saw conversing with one another after leaving the dock, spoke in that same language. In my dream, I tried to analyze the language. I asked myself, "Is he speaking Russian, Polish, Serbian, Slovak, or what?" I knew it was not German or a Romance language. Then what was it? After this analysis, I woke up and asked myself, "What did the priest say to me?" What is the meaning of this dream that had no ending?

The dream was of short duration, but the vivid image of the priest and his language haunted me for days as I tried to concentrate on my studies. Given my track record, I knew there had to be some significance to this mysterious dream yet to unfold.

After summer school, I returned to St. Irene's to begin the new school year. I looked forward to teaching the students I had had in first grade, now entering seventh grade, as well as music in the upper grades, and with the adult choir. When I arrived at the convent, Sister Adria, the principal was there to greet me. After unpacking my suitcase, I went outdoors to sweep the sidewalks in front of the convent. As I briskly swept debris and leaves from a previous night's storm, Sister Adria said, "Oh, here comes Father Michael down the street. He's probably coming to get his car parked in our garage. You haven't met the new assistant priest, so I'll introduce you to him."

By that time, the priest was in full view. I stopped sweeping. Still clutching the broom, I looked at him. There, before any introduction, I recognized the same priest I had seen in my dream. What a revelation! "Sister Avellino, this is Father Michael, our new assistant," Sister Adria said. "Father is from Poland and does not speak English as yet," she went on to say. He extended his hand as I reached out my arm, which seemed paralyzed, and tried to give him a warm welcome without words. He smiled, the same smile I saw in the dream, and in a ceremonial bow, released my hand. He then slowly walked down the driveway to get his car.

I liked the introduction without words and much feeling. A quote from Shakespeare's *Winter's Tale* flashed into my mind. "I like your silence, it the more shows off your wonder." I never revealed my dream to the sisters or anyone. This was only the beginning, I mused, of what was yet to come. Amid the mystery there was something sacred about this moment that I dared not question.

The following morning, I played the organ and Sister Charlette and I sang the seven o'clock Mass with Father Michael as celebrant. He spoke Latin beautifully, but did not sing the parts of the Mass assigned to the celebrant. That seemed strange to me. I could understand why he did not have a brief commentary on the Scripture readings of the day since he did not speak English.

I returned to the convent to eat breakfast before going to school to prepare for the upcoming school year. While I was eating, the pastor called Sister Adria. I overheard the conversation. "Yes, I'm sure one of the sisters would be happy to teach English to Father Michael," Sister Adria replied. "He knows seven languages?" she questioned. "Do you know anything about his background?" she asked the pastor. "Oh, so he's a history professor," she said. "Do you know where he taught?" There must have been a lengthy answer to that question. Finally, Sister Adria said, "I'll have one of the sisters begin teaching him today," and hung up the receiver.

When Sisters Charlette and Christoval came from upstairs, Sister Adria said to them, "The pastor just called and wants one of us to teach English to Father Michael. Would either of you be willing to teach him?" Both of them replied with an emphatic "No." Sister Adria said, "Well, I don't want to teach him either; I'll ask Sister Avellino," she said.

Little did Sister Adria know that I overheard the telephone conversation with the pastor and her asking the two sisters. When she came to me in the community room, she said, "Sister, I want you to begin English lessons with Father Michael today, if possible. He has to learn the language or he will not be of any assistance to Father Stier and this parish. I'll get some books for you on *English as a Second Language*, but you can begin with conversation until the books arrive," she said without any opening for me to reply. My initial thought was, how is he going to feel about my teaching him? I'm only 26 years old; he has to be near 50. The other sisters were more his age. Were they intimidated by him? If so, why? Do they know something I don't know, since I just arrived back from Milwaukee? I felt I had nothing to lose when I obediently accepted the challenge and did not verbally voice my concerns to Sister Adria. I had never taught English to a foreigner, but I felt confident I could do it. I also assumed that Father Michael would be highly motivated and conscientious in learning as fast as possible.

When we sisters walked to school, I stopped at the rectory and Father Stier came to the door. I told him I would be teaching English to Father Michael and that I wanted to arrange a time with him. He called Father Michael to the door and I began my first English lesson. I pointed to the clock, then held up two fingers and said, "English—two o'clock." Father Michael repeated the words after me and nodded his head assuring me he understood. Then I pointed to the convent, several blocks down the street, saying, "Convent—two o'clock." He again repeated the words and nodded. Then in Polish, he said, "Dziekuje" (Thank you). From that moment, I knew we were off to a good start.

Two o'clock arrived and Father Michael was at our doorstep. I greeted him, "Good afternoon," to which he replied with the same greeting in English. I had placed many objects on the dining room table to begin the lesson. As I held up each object, I said the word in English, and asked him to repeat the word: book, pencil, pen, magazine. After naming all the objects, we counted all of them. We went up to number 25, then reviewed all the names of the objects again. I was amazed! He missed naming two objects which he identified in Polish and went through the numbers without a mistake. I could immediately tell that he was a fast learner and someone who would challenge me after he learned English.

We worked intensely for one hour that first day. Then he spoke in Latin to me, and I actually surprised myself by remembering what I had learned in high school. I was able to get the main idea of what he tried to convey: namely, "I want to give the sermons in English in one month."

I certainly did not want to discourage his ambition, but felt this was an unrealistic goal. This also meant that I was the key person in helping him attain that goal. Would I have the time with teaching, organist and sacristy work? I made every effort to take time to teach Father. He adjusted his schedule to mine, especially after school had begun. We worked together for one to two hours daily and, by the time school started, he had made great progress. He not only was eager to learn, but we had fun in the process. I tried several times to trick him and was not always successful. We became competitive, which kept both of us on our toes.

By October, Father Michael gave brief homilies and read the announcements in English at Mass. He practiced with me first and then felt confident before the congregation. There were times he walked to the convent with me after school. Invariably, he would venture to the side of the street and pick certain weeds and inform me, "If war ever comes to this country, these are weeds you can eat." I would respond, "Father, you are in America, you need to forget your past." I later learned from him that one of the medical doctors in town gave him medication to dull his memory.

His past was difficult to forget. He shared with me that his family knew only war in Poland. His country was a corridor for all nations to use in time of war. He also was brainwashed by the Communists and fled to this country. His brother sought refuge in New Zealand. Apparently, his family owned the railroad system in Poland and this came under the scrutiny of the Communist leadership. I did not fully understand this problem because he was unable to communicate clearly in English at that time. I never approached this topic again because of the painful memories.

At one of his English classes, he told me he was having trouble with his car. I questioned him about where he bought the car and what seemed to be the problem. He was able to say "transmission and brakes" in English. I finally said, "Let's go to one of our parishioners and run a diagnostic test on the car," which we did. The mechanic said he purchased a "lemon" and that it was dangerous to drive. He also said to

Father, "You should never have bought the car before you could speak English." He suggested I go with Father Michael back to the dealer.

I was not happy about the suggestion, but I did not want Father Michael endangering his or someone else's life. To the car dealer we went. I was apprehensive about his driving the car there. I then asked Father Michael how he passed the driver's test without knowing English. He said, "I took the written test in Spanish since they did not have it in Polish or any other language I know." "How many languages do you know?" I asked. "Seven" was his reply. In driving down Roosevelt Road, I could see that he knew the rules of the road, so I did not want to interrogate him anymore.

The dealer was not happy to see the two of us, especially when I said, "You have taken advantage of this priest, who could not speak English at the time and we are here to return the car and get his money back." The dealer in a gruff tone said, "That's in violation of our policy. The deal was made and that was final." Then to my surprise, Father Michael spoke up and said, with a Polish accent and broken English, "I refuse to leave until I get the money back. This car is a lemon and a danger to others and me."

The dealer was shocked to hear Father Michael speak English. I was so proud of Father and realized for the first time that his English lessons with me had paid off. After bickering back and forth, the dealer threw up his arms in disgust, went to his desk and wrote out a check for the car to be returned.

When Father Michael and I walked out of the office and the dealer was not in sight, we both laughed aloud. I think it was more a release of tension rather than any humor in this dramatic scene. I praised Father for standing up for himself in English. Then he looked at me and was serious in asking: "Are we going to walk back to Warrenville?" It did not register with me that we needed a ride back home. I suggested we walk to the nearby McDonald's and I would call one of my choir members who lived in the area to come for us.

While we waited for the driver, I asked Father Michael if he knew enough about cars to purchase another one. His answer, "No, in Poland all cars were near death." Then I said, "I know nothing about cars either, so you will need someone else to go with you. There is a parent whose child is in St. Irene School I could ask. Do you feel comfortable with that?"

"Yes, I trust your judgment," he said.

Father Michael bought a second-hand gray-blue Chevrolet with only 120 miles. The widow who had owned it had a stroke and was no longer capable of driving. As a "thank you," he invited me to go with him to Morton Arboretum in Lisle, Illinois, and have an English lesson walking in the beauty of nature. Then with suppressed tears as I looked into his eyes, he said, "I miss my country, my friends, my family. I feel so alone."

How could I refuse the invitation? I welcomed the opportunity to walk in this haven of beauty and serenity especially in autumn—my favorite season. Most of all, I felt compassion for him. If a walk among the trees would lift his spirits, then I was happy to go with him. Sister Adria gave her permission.

The branches of the tall, stately trees arched over us as we began our walk down the path in silence. It was a meditation walk for both of us. I did not want to invade the stillness nor did he. We walked and walked. Silence. Peace. Love. "Let's sit on that bench under the oak tree," Father Michael finally said in a whispering voice. As we sat down, he said, "I would like to ask you a question."

"Yes, what is it?" I asked.

"When you first met me with a broom in your hand, why did you look at me in such a strange way? What were you thinking? I sensed something going on inside you," he calmly said as he looked me in the eye.

Just as I thought—when he learns English, look out! This was a question I had hoped he would never ask. I hesitated a moment and then said, "I had already seen you."

"Where did you see me?" he questioned.

"In a dream I had in July. You were getting off a ship and spoke to me in a language I did not recognize. I spent most of the dream analyzing the language. I couldn't figure out why you appeared to me," I said as I looked at his inquisitive blue eyes.

"How did the dream end?" he quickly asked.

"The dream had no ending. I awoke and was baffled by it, especially by dreaming in a foreign language," I said.

"What did I say to you?" he asked.

"I don't know, do you know?"

"I probably asked you for help since that was on my mind

123

coming over here on the ship," he said. "Do you believe in dreams?" he asked as he crossed his legs.

"Yes, certainly after this dream," I retorted. "How about you? Do you believe in dreams?" I asked him.

"Oh, yes, Scripture has many examples. Dreams are powerful and deeply spiritual," he responded.

I did not tell him that my prophetic dreams ended in tragedy or some great sorrow. Maybe this dream would have a happy ending I thought.

"Do you want to say anything else about the dream?" he asked. I said "no." I then said to him, "I'd like to ask you a question. Why don't you sing at Mass?"

"Good question," he said. "When I was in the seminary, they made fun of my singing, so I just refused to sing after that. I know I have a problem in my head," he said as he smiled and pointed to his forehead. "I'm no longer in the seminary, but I fear others will make fun of me," he said with a hint of anxiety in his voice.

"I'm going to help you overcome this fear and teach you to sing," I said with an assuring smile.

"You've been a good English teacher, so maybe you will be able to help me in singing," he said with hesitation and doubt.

"Let's try singing out here where only the trees will hear you," I said, trying to gently coax him.

He laughed and said, "If the branches start moving and the leaves start falling, you'll know they are laughing at me."

I sang "Dominus vobiscum" and asked him to sing it. He had difficulty with pitch. I sang different pitches on the vowel "o" and stayed on the pitch until he matched it. After several attempts, he sang "Dominus vobiscum" with me in tune. Then he sang it alone and I answered, "Et cum Spiritu tuo." Each time I am with you, we will practice another phrase," I told him. "Enough for today," I said; "you did very well."

(By Christmas, he had overcome his fear and sang the entire Mass. The first time he sang "Ite missa est" at a weekday Mass, I thought he was going to faint. Even one of the altar boys said he turned white and ran to get him a glass of cold water. Father Michael said to me later, "I consider singing the Mass as one of the great victories of my life, thanks to you.")

We slowly strolled back to the entrance of the arboretum to where he had parked his car. On the way, he saw mushrooms growing under a tree and went enthusiastically to pick them. I said, "Those mushrooms are poison. Why are you picking them?"

"Oh, no, not these; I know every species of mushrooms," he said. "These are good. I love mushrooms." He took them to the rectory to fix for supper and did not appear to be sick the next day.

I then asked him, "What did you do in Poland as a priest?"

"I taught history at the University of Warsaw and I taught at the Hague in the Netherlands. I was also a chaplain at one time at a women's prison," he nonchalantly said.

"Do you like teaching?" I asked. "I love it," he said as he dropped one of his mushrooms and I stooped to pick it up. He apologized that I dirtied my hands. Then he said, "I think I could begin teaching history and geography to the students in seventh and eighth grades. They would be able to understand my English, wouldn't they?"

"Yes, you have made remarkable progress in speaking and reading English. What about teaching religion?" I asked.

"No, I'm not a good theology teacher," he said.

The following week, Sister Adria and I invited Father to teach geography and history. He began the class at 1:00 p.m. The dismissal bell rang at 3:00 p.m. and all students remained in their seats, even those who were taking a bus. I finally told Father that the parents would worry about their children not coming home on time. The students in one accord said, "We want to stay until Father is finished teaching us about Russia."

Sister Adria said, "Father, ten more minutes." The students, Sister Adria and I were fascinated by his teaching, his stories, examples. He was truly a gifted teacher. Each week he focused on a different country and often dressed in the attire or brought something to show from the territory and displayed a map of the world.

At the next class, Father taught the students how to resist brainwashing. Sister Adria and I did not remain in the classroom. We thought he was going to finish the material on Russia but did not realize he would include the topic of Communism. When we returned to our classes, it was as if the students were drugged. They stared into space and were "out of it." Sister and I worked for almost a week to get these students back to normal.

Sister Adria said to him later, "Father, whatever you did in the classroom, please don't ever do this again to the children," and she told him the reaction of the students. He was apologetic and when I saw him later in the sacristy, he had tears in his eyes as he said, "I had to resist brainwashing by the Communists. I just felt they might need the techniques someday."

I said, "I know you meant well, Father, but these are children you are teaching, not adults." I often wondered what would have been my reaction had I remained in the classroom that afternoon.

Within several months, Father Michael had won the hearts and minds of, not only the children, but the parishioners. The lines at the confessional were twice the length of the pastor's. People came to his Masses just to hear his homilies. Once he learned English, he was able to wrap the Scriptures around human hearts. Even the Protestant ministers and their congregations requested his presence at some of their services and events. The people simply loved him and showered him with gifts and dinner invitations.

Every year on November 10th, the feast of St. Andrew Avellino, my nameday, I recall a special time with Father Michael. He was deeply grateful for my teaching him English and overcoming his fear of singing. That day he came to me with a gift that he, himself, had wrapped and a card of thanks he had written in English. When he handed me the gift, he wished me a Happy Nameday and was eager for me to open the package. I unwrapped the gift and the words "Delicacy: Chocolate Covered Grasshoppers and Ants" on a brightly decorated tin box with gold-trim glared at me. I kissed him on the cheek, the first I had ever shown him this kind of emotional response, and thanked him. I then said, "I know you drove into Chicago to get this precious gift." I looked at him and did not know how to say to him without hurting his feelings that there is no way I could eat grasshoppers and ants.

As I sat there looking at a grasshopper leg I felt nauseated. Never was I at a loss for words as at that moment. He immediately sensed my struggle and said to and for me, "You don't like chocolate covered grasshoppers and ants."

I replied, "No." Then with a smile, I said, "Apparently, you like this delicacy."

He said, "I love it, but never buy it for myself." I closed the box, held it with both hands, and gave it back to him saying, "This is my gift to you for being my best and brightest student and such a privilege and pleasure to teach. I want you to enjoy this delicacy."

He graciously accepted it, said "Thank you," opened it and began munching on the insects.

It was difficult for me to even watch him crunching on grasshoppers and ants, but it delighted me to see how he enjoyed my gift.

As an appreciation to the sisters for their support and help, Father Michael offered to cook a dinner for us in the convent kitchen. Sister Bernhilde was happy to have a break and let him take over in the kitchen. His main entre was smelts. That was something we had never had and we enjoyed them immensely. They were delicious. Since we did not have a dishwasher, the other sisters did the cleanup in the kitchen, while Father Michael and I went into the living room. He asked me to turn on the T.V. because he wanted to listen to a talk given by Nikita Khruschev, who was the General Secretary of the Communist Party of the Soviet Union. Khruschev, who delivered the speech in Russian, had an interpreter. As Father Michael listened to the speech, he was livid. I never saw him so angry.

"The interpreter has it all wrong in the translation," he said. "No wonder you Americans don't get your stories straight!" he said with such vehemence. I saw a side of the kind, gentle Father Michael that I had never witnessed before. Thereafter, I always avoided the topic of Communism.

One Sunday morning after the Feast of the Epiphany, which Father Michael considered a much greater feast than Christmas and really celebrated, I walked into the sacristy to prepare for Mass. Father was deathly ill and was determined to celebrate Mass. I insisted he go back to the rectory and tell the pastor. I also said, "If Father Stier can't celebrate the Mass, I will call one of the Benedictine priests."

Father Michael said, "I am saying the Mass!"

I finally gave in, but said "We will not have a High Mass."

I sat in the front pew and watched him turn green when he distributed communion. I thought he was going to collapse as he looked at me several times. After he turned to the congregation to give the final blessing and said "Ite Missa est," he keeled over and lay prostrate on the altar steps. I ran up to him, asked the servers to bring me a wet towel and started to remove his vestments. Three men ran up to assist and one ran to the rectory to call for an ambulance since there was no phone in the church.

Within a short time, the paramedics arrived and revived Father. I wanted him to go to Central DuPage Hospital near Warrenville. Father Michael insisted he go to Resurrection Hospital in Chicago, which the Polish sisters owned and operated. I, as well as the paramedics, did not think he would make it going that distance, but we had no time to argue. As the paramedics carried him out on the stretcher, he said to me as he grabbed my hand, "Remember to bury me in the vestments I showed you. And thanks for all your help." Previously, he had indicated to me that if he died while in the parish, he wanted to be buried in the vestments he had placed in a box in one of the closets. At that time, his death never entered my mind, but it certainly did at this moment.

As soon as he arrived at Resurrection Hospital, the doctors determined he had a prostate problem and kidney failure and did immediate surgery. We received word that within another hour, he would have died. I gave a sigh of relief. Many parishioners and the sisters prayed for him as he remained in the hospital after surgery to recover. Bishop Blanchette then sent him to Hot Springs, Arkansas, for six weeks to regain his health.

While he was enjoying the hot mineral baths, I had my students compile a book: *This Is Your Life*. One of my seventh grade boys was gifted in drawing hands. On each page, Christopher drew the development of Father Michael's hands beginning as a baby through his ordination with his hands raising the host, the chalice, giving absolution, etc. The class then wrote something significant about him at the various stages of life that the hands signified. The students were thrilled with their final production, but no one was more elated as I to see this sacred, memorable book done by the students. Several girls found a box, wrapped it in beautiful paper and then went to FedEx to ship it.

When Father Michael returned to the parish, he came to the classroom and thanked the students for the book he would treasure for life. He said, "Reading that book contributed to my healing more than any of the treatments."

Life was without any major catastrophes in the parish for several months. It gave me time to heed the words of Doctor Texter to "listen to my body; the body doesn't lie." I felt I was getting back in the same rut as before when I noticed a discomfort in my esophagus, Nature's warning signal to me. I took some leisure time out for myself while still teaching. Periodically, Father Michael would say, "You look so tired. I want you to take these vitamins," which I did. When I had a terrible cold, he gave me a tonic that he concocted and said, "You must take this each day, Sister." I did, and recovered.

The month of December seemed to come more quickly that year, 1960. I prepared the adult choir for Advent and Christmas, as well as the upper grade students. On a bleak December day, as I was laying out vestments in the priests' sacristy for the following day's Mass, Father Michael came to see me. I could see he was serious and deliberate in what he was about to say. "Sister, tomorrow I'm going to see the bishop."

There was a pause, so I asked, "Why?"

"Because I'm in love with you and I'm asking to be transferred," he said.

"Transferred?" I asked, gasping for breath.

"Yes," he said, I've prayed and thought about this. You are more needed in this parish than I, so I will choose to leave."

"What are you going to say to the bishop?" I asked.

"I'm telling the truth—I'm in love with you," he firmly stated.

"But do you have to take such drastic measures? You've had enough trauma in your life. Why are you inviting more change—you've only been here one and a half years? You are too hard on yourself, Father Michael," I boldly stated.

"Yes," he said, "all my life I've experienced nothing but war, and now I'm in war with myself."

The tears started to trickle down my face. I held his hand and said, "I love you, too, Father." I looked at him and he gazed at me with a soft and gentle look. I felt his heart and mind were feuding as he pensively looked at me and slowly walked out of the sacristy.

The following day, Father Michael went to see Bishop Blanchette. Several days later when Father came to the sacristy to vest for Mass, he showed me the letter dated December 12, 1960, the Feast of Our Lady of Guadalupe. The bishop assigned him to a parish in the southern part of the diocese as pastor and where he would utilize his English as well as several other languages. He said to me, "The bishop was pleased that I could speak English so well. I told him that Sister Avellino, the woman I'm in love with, taught me. How could I not have strong feelings toward this woman? She did so much for me. I love her,

129

but I can no longer deal with my passions as a celibate."

"Did I do something wrong, Father?" I asked.

"Oh no, no no," he said. "Don't you feel guilty. This is the man in me and my passions that I'm having to deal with," he said as if he were chastising himself.

Quoting St. Augustine, I said, "God is not disturbed by any passions."

"You must not have read far enough in his *Confessions*," he said with a bit of laughter. "His passions haunted him all his life and he has haunted the Church with his theology that everybody accepts as gospel. Try quoting someone with more credibility," he challenged me.

I thought for a minute and said, "Hildegarde of Bingen said 'The truly holy person welcomes all that is earthly,' and Mechtilde of Magdeburg wrote: 'Do not disdain your body. For the soul is just as safe in its body as in the Kingdom of Heaven.'"

Father chuckled. "Sometimes I feel the women mystics had greater insights than the men. However, Thomas Aquinas taught that human virtues are actually contained in the passions and Meister Eckhart taught that 'no deed is accomplished without passion.'"

These were the little games we sometimes played in our more competitive moments in English class, but I dare say in this situation, it was for comic relief.

"I can tell you are happy about your appointment," I said.

"Yes, I am. I never thought of becoming a pastor. That parish has been without a priest for over a year. Other priests have had to fill in, so the bishop said I was an answer to his prayers," he said.

"I know you will be a great pastor. You'll even be able to have a High Mass now that you are able to sing. 'Singing is twice praying,'" I said, quoting St. Augustine again.

"I'm getting the impression you like Augustine," he said.

"Not really," I said, "but he's better than Thomas a Kempis, who considered passions a curse rather than a blessing."

Then I saw his mood change. He looked at me and said in a solemn tone, "I will always love you and never forget you. You have made me a greater man and better priest."

My smile was cloaked in sadness as I said, "Thank you," and went back to the choir loft.

I went through the motions of playing the organ and singing. I was happy there were few people at Mass that day. My thoughts were on Father Michael. By December 20th, he was to be in his new parish, which meant there was no time for a parish farewell. Thus, during Mass I planned a program with the upper grades. I went through the list of songs they had already learned that would be fitting for the occasion. I decided that Donald would emcee the program. I felt good about the plans and then wondered if I could pull this off emotionally in front of the students. And what would be Father's response?

After Mass, I went to my classroom. "By heaven, I do love and it hath taught me to rhyme and to be melancholy," I thought to myself as I took solace in Shakespeare's *Love's Labour's Lost*. I then thought of my love for Father Michael and how much I would miss him.

> His love was an eternal plant;
> Whereof the root was fixed in virtue's ground
> The leaves and fruit maintained with beauty's sun.
> (Henry VI, Part III)

I said not a word to Sister Adria, the other sisters, teachers, and parishioners. This news had to be given by the pastor and there was so little time. Father Stier told the sisters the following day, so that gave me the freedom to plan a small farewell with the school children. Everyone was shocked at the news, including the pastor, as they were all trying to figure out why. Father Stier concluded that the bishop was in dire straits when he said, "I understand the plight of the bishop."

Father Michael took time to go to all classrooms to say goodbye. When he came to the upper grades, he was escorted downstairs to the hall where the students were in formation to sing. The emcee welcomed him and expressed appreciation for all he had taught them and for his kindness and love of them. As I played the piano, they sang: "You'll Never Walk Alone;" "I'll Walk with God;" "Vaya Con Dios" (May God Go with You). He loved classical music so I played Beethoven's "Moonlight Sonata" to soothe his aching heart. Sister Adria told me later he wiped away tears during the whole performance. She was not able to see the tears that trickled down my face. I could not release my hands from the piano keys to wipe them away.

I dreaded saying my final goodbye to Father Michael. He came into the sacristy as I made preparations for the next day's Mass, which Father Stier was to celebrate, since Father Michael was to leave early the next morning for a funeral in his new parish. He looked at me and for the first time embraced and kissed me. Both of us held each other and sobbed. It was as if we did not want to let go of one another. There were no spoken words—reminiscent of when we first met. I finally broke the silence by asking, "May I write or visit you?"

He replied, "No, it has to be a clean break. That's in your best interest as well as mine."

I hugged him again and gave a final kiss. With eyes filled with tears, I said, "We now know the ending of my dream."

He squeezed me tightly to his heart: "Goodbye, thank you, God be with you." Now, when I reflect on that sacramental moment, the words of the Irish poet and philosopher, John O'Donohue, resonate deep within me:

> Love is the most real form of human presence. It is the threshold
> where divine and human presence ebb and flow into each other.

Eight years later, I traveled with another sister to a workshop and went through the town where he was sent. We were one block away from Father Michael's rectory and church. I asked Sister if she would mind if I stopped at the rectory for just a brief time. She was most agreeable and waited in the car for me. I rang the rectory doorbell, figuring eight years was a long time. He opened the door and was delightfully surprised to see me in a short habit and my hair showing. He embraced me and said, "Don't tell me you've had another dream!" He was elated to see me looking well and happy. No tears were shed at this encounter. I saw him happy, well-adjusted to America and a real shepherd to his flock.

In the entrance, I noticed his large world map that almost covered the entire wall, just as he had had in his study at St. Irene's. I pointed to the map and said, "Your love and commitment are to the whole world, not just to me." He smiled, thanked me for stopping in, and gave me his blessing.

Father Michael died some years later. I read the obituary in the diocesan paper and prayed that the angels led him into paradise. "Requiescat in pace."

Now at this time of my life, what are my reflections on this rich life experience that had plunged both of us into dealing with our human sexuality? First of all, it would have been sad for me to have gone through life without ever knowing Father Michael. To know him was to love him. I deeply respect and honor him for his discipline, fidelity to his priesthood, and the difficult decision he made. In his case, he said "no" for a better "yes." However, I cannot refrain from looking at this experience in a much larger context: namely, the Catholic Church's stance on celibacy. It is in the shadow of my experiences that I believe many priests would be much better priests if they were married. Why does mandatory celibacy have to be part of the package deal of becoming a priest? Is celibacy essentially more perfect than married love? Some priests are called to ministry, but not to celibacy. Isn't it hypocritical that the Church allows Protestant ministers who have converted to Catholicism to be ordained priests and remain married?

I have also experienced that celibacy contributes to clericalism—a feeling by clergy that they are separate and above everyone else. The rules don't apply to them. Mandatory celibacy also restricts the availability of Eucharist to the people of God. Why are we merging two and three parishes because of a priest shortage? There are solutions to this problem. And finally, celibacy was not instituted by Jesus. St. Paul thought the end of the world was near and advised celibacy for those who could live it. It was a witness to the end times being at hand. The monks in the fourth century practiced celibacy as a witness also to the end times and as a form of asceticism. Gradually, local councils imposed celibacy on diocesan clergy. Many of the bishops were first monks. In the 12th century, celibacy was imposed on the Western clergy to prevent the squabbles over what the family owned and what the parish owned. What a sad commentary on the Church for having the origins of mandatory celibacy rooted in power and money.

Optional celibacy will not solve all the problems. It may well create other problems. In Protestant churches there is no such thing as optional celibacy. Most of the congregations I am familiar with require a minister to be married. They are looking for a stable, family person, not one who is still dating. If the minister is not married, it is assumed he is homosexual and is often subject to prejudice. Thank God, there is now more tolerance and acceptance of gays. What will be the status of homosexual priests who presently are safely couched under the veil of celibacy? What about a man who is called to the single life? I merely ask the questions.

What about my personal life as a celibate and one who has embraced the vow of chastity? This has not always been easy for me.

Father Michael is only one example. As I reflect on life, I think the energy of my sexuality was and is directed into other channels: namely, teaching, music, art, writing. These channels, as I analyze them from my perspective, allow me to have life-enriching creativity that compensates for the lack of intimacy. This creative energy ushers me into the potential of wholeness that I might never have achieved otherwise. Many of my relationships at varying levels of friendship sustain me in a life devoid of that "one special person." In fact, I often felt that had I married, I probably would have struggled in remaining faithful to one person. I was and still am a woman of diversity even in relationships.

Another aspect of celibacy I experience is that my friendships with married persons of the opposite sex are not filled with threat to that person's marriage. Consequently, these relationships over the years have been rich, enduring, and life-giving. As a celibate, I have had the freedom in relationships that most married women do not have.

Having said all of this, I realize celibacy is an option for a small minority. That is why I am for optional celibacy in the priesthood. For some people, celibacy is one way, and the best path to human wholeness, if not for a lifetime commitment as I have made, then at least for certain periods of one's life.

I feel that the whole topic of human sexuality has yet to be explored. Not all the questions have been asked. Probably Bishop John Shelby Spong has courageously asked the most questions in our culture and our times. The answers have yet to evolve. It's a subject people are reticent to speak about, yet the gift of sexuality is something we all have in common.

It is time that scholars devote attention to this topic and begin serious dialogue about it. Reflection and discussion are urgently called for on a topic of such moral and pastoral significance. It becomes more apparent each day as one reads the papers and watches T.V., to say nothing of social media, that profound changes in sexual attitudes and behavior patterns are prevalent in America and elsewhere. This leads to serious questions regarding the adequacy of traditional Catholic teachings and pastoral responses to sexual matters.

Julian of Norwich, a 14th century mystic, explicitly states: "As regards our sensuality, it can rightly be called our soul because of the union it has with God. God is in our sensuality." Our sensuality, our sexuality are founded "in nature, in compassion, and in grace."

Chapter XI

My Mother's Death

The telephone rang on Friday morning, September 1, 1989. Mom, in the kitchen preparing dinner for my father and me, asked me to take the call. I hesitated a moment, wondering who it could be. What could it be? Is someone inviting us for a Labor Day weekend party?

Deep within, I knew it had to be my brother Charles calling from his office in Jefferson City.

"The doctor's report is not good news. Mom has a tumor in her pancreas. I asked the doctor how long he thought she would live. "Four weeks," he said.

"Four weeks!"

Mom in her early 80s
Photo courtesy: Margaret E. (Stiefermann) Powers

I repeated with a disbelieving tremor. I heard my brother's deep sigh. "Do you want me to tell Mom now or would you prefer waiting until I come home this evening?" Charles asked. I braced myself and said, "I will tell her now. It's hard to keep a secret from Mom."

By this time, Mom had walked into the hall; she looked at me as I put down the receiver. There was a dramatic silence. I slowly accompanied her into the bedroom as I tried to think of how and what I was going to say. She sat on the bed. I put my arms around her. "Mom, I have sad news for you and for all of us. Charles just called and said your doctor's report indicates you have a tumor in the pancreas." Tears streamed down my cheeks as I continued, "And Mom, according to Dr. Meier, you have four weeks to live."

I was so relieved when I had all the words out that it did not occur to me how such a death sentence would strike anyone, let alone my mother. But without a tear or a moment's hesitation, she said, "Barbaralie, I am eighty-five years old; I have lived a long life. I am ready to die." Adjusting the pillows, she casually added, "So, I'm dying of pancreatic cancer—I've got to die of something."

I hugged her and said, "How beautiful, Mom. Four weeks is hard for me to accept, but I honor and respect what you are saying. And I certainly do not want you to linger and suffer." I reached for the nearby Kleenex.

She looked at me: "When I came into the world, everyone rejoiced. Now that I am going back to where I came from, you are sad. Please don't cry—I'll still be with you."

"Mom, I know you'll never leave us. And really, what would we do without you?" I joked as I prepared for the next statement. "I assume you want Charles and me to call all of the family tonight."
"Yes," she said, "and I want time alone with each of you, so space the visits accordingly.

I turned around. There in the doorway stood my ninety-two year old father. He looked at Mom and me as he walked toward us. I immediately stood up and put my arms around him. "Daddy, the diagnosis of Mom's condition is not what you would like to hear. She has a tumor in the pancreas."

"Is this cancer?" he asked.

"In all probability, yes. Doctor Meier gives Mom four weeks to live," I said.

Daddy's blue eyes looked into the brown eyes of his wife. What was communicated at that moment could have been done only in the language of silence. "I do not want you to suffer any more; we must accept what is," my father bravely said. His head offered all the right things, but his heart was not in sync. He cried aloud. Mom and I put our arms around him.

"Don't cry, August; I'll always take care of you. It won't be long until I call you home, too," she said. At that moment, I felt I needed someone's arms around me.

As the three of us tried to step back into the mainstream of life, Mom was the only one who seemed to achieve it. "Well, I will finish preparing dinner and after we eat, I'll do what I've always done—watch the soap opera."

Life continued at its normal pace for Mom, but not for the rest of us. On Saturday afternoon, my father and I were sitting in the living room discussing what our lives would be like after Mom had gone. As our glance traveled through the dining room into the kitchen, we saw her making a pie, cleaning off the counter, stacking the dishwasher. Daddy turned toward me and said, "Look at her. And she's supposed to be dead in four weeks? It's incredible!"

As unbelievable as it was, I knew certain things needed to be accomplished. That evening I asked hesitatingly, "Mom, what hymns would you like sung at your funeral Mass?"

"Well, you know we had 'How Great Thou Art' for our Golden Wedding anniversary. I think it would be appropriate for my funeral too," she answered with a little smile as if she were happy. "And everyone in the parish knows the song 'Be Not Afraid'."

That prompted me to ask, "Mom, are you afraid to die?"

"Afraid? No. I've spent my whole life preparing for this moment. We are born to die, Barbaralie." How profound, I thought. Mom, who had only a grade school education, understood that the paradox of living is dying. There we sat—the two of us planning all the details of a funeral just as we might prepare for a wedding. I asked myself several times, "What is it we are really celebrating?"

Mom's enthusiasm continued to overwhelm me. "I want the gospel story about Christ saying to his apostles, 'My peace I leave with you' when He was ready to leave them and ascend into heaven," she said. This is not one of the gospels usually selected for a traditional Catholic funeral, I thought, but if this is what Mom wants, so be it.

"What kind of flowers would you like on the coffin?" I ventured. "Your daughters will come home and have their ideas of what it should be, but what do you want?"

She thought for a few moments. Her sunken eyes looked at me as she said, "White roses are my favorite, but mix pink ones in to match my Golden Jubilee dress that I want to be buried in." There was a slight pause. "Put seven birds in the casket bouquet. You know how I love birds, especially the cardinal. After the ceremony in the cemetery, each of you take a bird and every time you hear a singing bird, know that I am present."

After all the preparations had been made, I embraced Mom and said, "I pray that when my time comes, I can be as calm and courageous as you. Your resignation is strength to me. I love you, Mom."

That 1989 Labor Day weekend was over. I packed my suitcase, said goodbye to my parents and traveled to Milwaukee. There I tried to arrange my work so that I could go back home again to be with Mom and Daddy. I worked rapidly to prepare the liturgy and a cover design for the Mass booklet, a memorial card, and a "thank you" card for those many people who would express their sympathy to the family. After rearranging meetings, canceling appointments and putting final touches on a manuscript to be published, I boarded the Amtrak train on September 14. All the while, I could hear the clock ticking louder and louder. I felt angry because I had no control over time. I felt helpless because there was nothing I could do to stop the inevitable, and I was angry at myself for not being able to take Mom's suffering away.

I found myself bargaining with God on that long train ride— pleading for death to be slowed down to accomplish all that needed to be done. I wanted more time to love Mom and for her to experience it. Then I prayed that Mom die quickly and felt misgivings in asking for the death of my mother. I began to realize what a poor bargainer I was, that this was so contrary to the beautiful example Mom was teaching us in facing death honestly and courageously. As I peered out the window at the miles of flat Illinois land, I felt like a stranger to myself. Going home because Mom was dying was a new experience for me. The ride seemed desolate and unending. "My God, give me strength," I said as the conductor finally announced Jefferson City.

Charles met me at the station and as we drove on the winding highways to Frankenstein, he updated me concerning Mom's condition. Her color was now yellow and she was considerably weaker than when I had last seen her. "But," he added, "her spirit and attitude have not changed. She is amazing. All who come to visit her are inspired by her smile, graciousness and concern for them." He also told me Maggie and Betty, our sisters who each had had their time with Mom, called her a "valiant woman" when they witnessed her rapport with visitors and with them.

The stars peeked out and the full moon leaned gently on the hill near our home as we pulled up to the yard gate. Mom had often entertained us as children with made-up stories about the moon, stars, galaxies and Milky Way. To her dying day, the phases of the moon had a special attraction. As we walked on the sidewalk leading to the front door, I sensed immediately that Mom must be worse. I did not see her white curly hair through the living room window. The rocking chair she always occupied was empty. Daddy walked onto the porch to welcome us. My sister Kathleen and her husband Bill, from Gatlinburg, greeted me as I entered the dining room. The hollowness of words brought a haunting silence.

I slowly made my way to the bedroom where Mom—waiting to see me—was propped on pillows. She smiled as I clasped her hand and kissed her. "I'm happy to see you, Barbaralie. Did you have something to eat?" she asked.

"Yes, Mom," I replied, "but I must admit I missed your fried chicken and those fresh garden vegetables you always prepared for me." We visited briefly and I wished her a peaceful night.

The next morning, Kathleen and Bill said goodbye to Mom and returned to Gatlinburg, knowing that the next time they returned would be for her funeral. After they had gone, Kathleen's daughter Maureen from Baltimore called to inquire about Mom and to confirm her time with her grandmother. As she gave me the airline schedule, I quickly wrote down the details to report to Mom because Maureen was the only family member who had not yet visited her. "Please tell Maureen that next weekend will be too late; she must come this weekend."

Who could challenge such certitude? Not I. I told Maureen she should plead with the airlines for a flight as soon as possible. Two days later Maureen was at the bedside of her grandmother, drinking in her wisdom and grateful that Mom had insisted she come sooner.

My sister Theresa, a nurse, also came that weekend to assist in caring for Mom at home. We had anticipated needing Theresa's skills when Mom became bedridden. Though she looked like a dying woman with her frail, slender body and yellow-orange skin, Mom did not act like someone who was about to draw her last breath. Her voice was strong; her lungs and heart functioned well. She was able to sit up to eat and to walk to the bathroom with assistance. After much discernment, we decided that Theresa should return to her work in St. Louis on Monday, and Charles and I would inform her when conditions became worse.

On Wednesday evening, my father, sister-in-law Mary, her twelve-year-old daughter Ann, and I gathered around Mom and prayed the rosary together. Mom fingered every bead and prayed aloud each "Hail Mary." After the rosary, she asked us to pray from her prayer book—prayers she had said daily.

From my childhood, I remember Mom praying the Litany of Loretto by memory every night after the family rosary. It always amazed me that she could go through an entire litany without getting stuck or mixed up. Periodically, my sisters and I checked a prayerbook to see if she was saying that litany in proper sequence. We didn't ever catch her making a mistake, and even in her dying moments, her memory served her well.

After the rosary that evening, Ann approached Grandma and said goodbye. Mom took her by the hand and smiled at her. "Don't you have homework to do?"

"Yes," Ann replied.

"Don't study too hard, Ann," Mom cautioned as she squeezed her grandchild's hand. Ann, a sensitive girl, realizing that this could be her final goodbye, cried as she left the bedroom.

On Thursday of that week, we could see Mom was growing weaker. My sister-in-law and I decided to call Theresa at 3 p.m. She was relieved to get the call. "Mom has been on my mind all day. I somehow felt you needed me. My suitcase is packed and I can still make the 5:20 p.m. train if I rush."

Two hours after we had called Theresa, Daddy and I accompanied Mom to the bathroom as we had always done. When she stepped into the bathroom, I felt her swaying; as she sat on the stool, she became dead weight. Her eyes rolled back; her head slumped. There was no sign of life. I looked at my dad and said, "Mom is dead; Mom is dead." We both started to cry. I told Daddy to hold her while I called Mary, who was attending a meeting in town. I dialed the telephone as if I were blindfolded. "Mary, come quickly; we need your help."

When I returned to the bathroom, Daddy was bewildered. He said, "I don't know what happened, but Mom came back to life again." By that time, Mary had arrived and the three of us helped Mom to bed. She was extremely weak. We later jokingly said, "Mom would never have wanted it said that she died sitting on the toilet; that's why she came back to life again."

From then on she became bedridden, but she remained alert and in good humor even though time was closing in on her. We did everything we could to keep her happy, even though it seemed outlandish to us. When she requested spareribs and sauerkraut, we gave them to her. A friend had given her homemade raspberry jelly which she relished to her last day.

After Theresa arrived that evening, Mom insisted that we should not interrupt our sleep to care for her, but we disobeyed her order. She took little medication: phenobarbital to help her sleep and a pain pill reluctantly. Never one to take pills, why should she do so now? Several times she asked for Imodium A-D, an antidiarrheal over-the-counter drug, which she did not really need, but claimed it relaxed her digestive system. When I told her how sorry I was she had to suffer, she quickly replied, "Jesus Christ also suffered."

Friday, September 22, was the day. Just three weeks earlier, Doctor Meier said Mom had only four weeks to live. Did that mean only one week was left? Even the sunrise seemed vague and indecisive, appearing to question the same thing. I asked Mom if she wanted me to call Father Walsh to cancel his bringing Communion to her because she had been spitting up brownish blood. "Oh, no. I want to receive," she said. Her deep faith, devotion and her smile inspired Father Walsh, my father, Theresa and me as we shared in her final Communion.

Shortly after the priest left, she asked Theresa and me if she should be taken to the hospital.

"Why?" was our reply.

"Maybe it's too hard on you to care for me at home," she said.

"Mom, we wouldn't think of sending you to the hospital. It is a privilege caring for you," Theresa said.

"You cared for us as children when we were sick. Nothing was too much for you. Let us now minister to you," I said as I touched her cold hands. She smiled and offered no resistance. I knew she was happy with our response. I sensed she knew this was to be her last day on earth and she was concerned about our attitude toward her dying at home. Would it disturb Daddy and us thereafter to walk into that bedroom where she had died?

At four o'clock that afternoon, Mom asked my father to lie in bed beside her. During the past three weeks, Daddy often had sat at Mom's bedside in silence and prayer. It was edifying to observe the silent love between them. Now she was asking him to lie beside her. Daddy looked at her in a puzzled manner, but promptly removed his shoes and honored her request. Mom clasped his hand tightly. What a beautiful model to Theresa, Charles and me as we witnessed the bond of love and fidelity of almost sixty years of marriage. This was Mom's way of fulfilling her marriage vows: "In sickness and in health, till death do us part."

I didn't want to cry, but no amount of will power could stop the tears. We began to pray aloud, "Holy Mary, Mother of God, pray for us sinners now and at the hour of our death." How often she had heard and said that prayer during her life. The answer to her plea seemed only breaths away.

Theresa monitored her breathing and with her eyes communicated to us that Mom was getting weaker. At one crucial moment, Mom closed her eyes and stopped breathing. We thought she was dead and started to cry. She opened her eyes, startled to see us in tears. With great ease, she raised her thin arms, spread them apart in priestly gesture and, as she looked at each of us, said: "Peace, peace be to all of you. My peace I leave with you."

We continued to pray aloud and Mom prayed with us. Periodically she said, "Let's just have silence now," and closed her eyes. When she wanted us to continue praying, she opened them. We used one of those opportunities to thank her for all she had done for us; we asked her forgiveness for any hurts we had caused, and we told her how much we loved her. Of all the Mother's Day cards we'd sent Mom over the years, none could compare with this bedroom scene where we each expressed in our own way that she was the most beautiful mother in the world. Life and death were brought together for us during her last hours on earth. She taught us not only how to live, but also how to die. Mom in turn, thanked us, forgave us, asked for our forgiveness and anointed us with her love. As I listened to her dying words, I regretted there was no tape recorder or video to enshrine her voice and sentiments forever.

At one of the times Mom's eyes were closed, I reflected on the previous three weeks. I had learned the certainty of death with great reluctance. My need to live is so great that even a fatal illness such as pancreatic cancer did not register as a sign of approaching death. I began to comprehend that part of my anger and bargaining with God was because I did not want to die. Yet, sooner or later I thought, I have to face the inevitable truth of my own dying. Would I be able to face death as Mom is? I also realized that resurrection had not been an experience of my heart until I was privileged to be with my mother during her fatal illness.

All the while we prayed and dialogued with Mom, my father was like a still life lying at her side. Because of his hearing loss, he was unable to understand anything being said. Yet, somehow he knew and sensed what was happening. Mom's final expression of love and farewell could be understood by anyone. She grasped each one's hand and squeezed it with such strength and finality that I felt an electric charge travel through my entire arm. No words were spoken. Her breathing became deeper and more stressed. I began praying, and then did a visualization in a soft tone of voice to help her make the transition from this life to the next. Theresa kept close watch on her pulse and breathing, while Charles, her only son, stood like a soldier on guard.

Mom went into a coma. I continued to pray and affirm her while holding her hand. Looking at the clock on the night stand, I saw that it was 8:20 p.m. The autumn equinox—my mother's favorite season—came in almost unnoticed. Mom died at 8:30 p.m. The world to me at that moment became eternally divided into before and after.

After the funeral was over and everyone had gone, Charles and I went for a walk down the country road in front of our parents' home. On that late afternoon, we saw a pink hue over the western rim of the earth. A cool breeze lapped our faces as many bluebirds sang and flitted to and fro. It was a moment of rare immutable joy—a moment for which I felt grateful to Life and to Death.

Chapter XII

My Wisdom Years

Most people can't wait until they retire. If the truth be known, I did not look forward to retirement. I enjoyed working in the art gallery. My fear was when I retire, what am I to do? In our society, people routinely ask what work we do after they ask our name. What will I say to them when my identity is no longer attached to what I do? Who am I in my retirement years? Will I go from being something to being nothing in a social system in which positions, recognition and work are the center of life? These were the questions that ultimately exposed the depth of my spirituality.

Fortunately, I read Sister Joan Chittister's book, *The Gift of Years: Growing Older Gracefully* and gained many insights on the aging process, which helped prepare me for retirement. On the blurb of the cover of her book it reads:

> She invites us to embrace older age as a natural part of life that is both active and contemplative, productive and reflective and deeply rewarding. She encourages us to cherish the blessings of aging and to overcome its challenges.

That summarized well for me the message of her book. I realized after reading the *Gift of Years* that I was entering a unique time of my life, perhaps the most special I was yet to experience. This is a time of wisdom, freedom, and wealth of another kind that I looked forward to.

Besides Sister Joan's book, another significant thing happened in my religious community that made retirement attractive to me. The School Sisters of St. Francis built on convent grounds in the heart of historic Layton Boulevard neighborhood in Milwaukee, a 72 apartment assisted living complex for laity and religious ages 62 and up. This beautiful facility called Maria Linden offers quality, adaptable apartments that allow residents to age in place. It offers the comforts of home with the security of around-the-clock staff to help when needing care assistance. At this time, I am of sound mind and body and do not require supportive services.

Every evening during the summer, I enjoy the quiet beauty of the meticulously maintained gardens. During the winter months, as well as in all the seasons, I walk the long corridors to the historic building, which also has charming apartments. In that section of the building there are more long corridors that lead to the dining room, art gallery, and chapel. In addition to the exercise, it is an aesthetic walk, because the corridors on all floors exhibit original paintings by our sisters.

The residents at Maria Linden enjoy numerous amenities as arts and crafts rooms, a health and wellness suite, fitness center, private consultation rooms, on-site hair salon/barber, business center with free internet services, and several cozy gathering spaces for friendship and entertainment. Another added feature are guest suites for visiting family and friends.

Why was this facility named Maria Linden? The roots of the School Sisters of St. Francis are embedded in Erlenbad, Gemany, which is near the site of the Maria Linden Shrine. Sister Rita Eble, vice-president of our international congregation, gives the following account.

> The history of pilgrimages to the Mother of God at Maria Linden in Ottersweier is over 500 years old. Legend has it that a picture of Mary, which had been placed in the cavity of a linden tree was overgrown by the tree bark and thus preserved from plundering nomadic hordes during a time of war. One evening, after peace and order had been restored in the country, a shepherd girl heard lovely singing that seemed to come from the tree. After she experienced the singing several times she told her father about it. The father, believing that the tree was under a magic spell, set out to cut it down. But no sooner had he touched the linden tree with his ax then the bark that had kept the picture hidden fell off, and he saw the likeness of Mary looking straight at him. News of this miraculous event spread quickly throughout the region and people were coming from near and far to see the miracle and to honor Mary in the picture. The gentry of Windeck had a chapel built next to the linden tree in which the picture was placed.

> In 1484 the Bishop of Strasbourg, whose diocese then included the Ortenau region, approved the building of a church in the place "where the Virgin Mary, Mother of God, has already revealed herself through miracles." Thus, through the magnanimity and generosity of the pilgrims, a beautiful church was erected in honor of Mary and the triune God (high altar). Since those early days, many people have come to this holy place, where they have entrusted their concerns to Mary, the Mother of Life.

It was at this shrine that Mother Alexia Hoell, foundress of the School Sisters of St. Francis in America in 1874, often went to pray. The sisters in our European province still frequent the shrine today.

I moved into Maria Linden on February 2, 2013. My one bedroom, one bath apartment on third floor features an open concept area containing a full-sized kitchen, snack bar, and living room. I arranged the living room with a love seat, winged back chair, antique chair, all

Maria Linden, an independent and assisted living complex for sisters and laity
Photo courtesy: Sister Alice Feather

in off-white, a cherry wood bookcase, television and small lap-top desk in black. There are two end tables on either side of the love seat with antique lamps. On the glass-topped coffee table is a large crystal lotus flower with a seven-inch LED candle in it. This provides a radiant setting for meditation. The beautiful paintings and the white-lady sculpture placed in front of a large window give the open area a classical look. Above the love seat is an inspiring Spanish-framed print of El Greco's "La Virgen de la Buena Leche" (The Virgin of Good Milk), which I purchased at Museo de El Prado in Madrid in 1976. It's my favorite depiction of the Virgin Mary; where I go it goes.

The bath features a built in vanity closet, linen cabinet and large shower with a padded seat. The non-skid floor is a safety feature in a bathroom large enough to accommodate a wheelchair.

The unit also includes a full-sized washer and dryer. I had never had a washer and dryer previously. I found myself treating them like toys—washing clothes that did not even need washing. There also is a heated garage—no more sliding across a parking lot to remove snow and ice from my car.

What do I appreciate most about Maria Linden? At this stage of my life, I enjoy the space for quiet meditation and contemplation. I have the best of both worlds—my desire for community interaction and activity, and the solitude and privacy of my apartment. After years of living in apartments with neighbors' stereos and boom boxes blasting, late-night parties, domestic fights, I'm happy to be in a safe place surrounded by peace and quiet. Added to the peacefulness, the apartment is filled with light, even on a dreary day.

Why am I making a big deal of my environment? I am a firm believer that adjusting and balancing the flow of energy within one's home does powerfully and effectively influence the course of a person's life. Besides having a bent toward artistry and beauty, I have been influenced by Eastern philosophy, having studied Tai Chi, Qigong, Taoism, Feng Shui. I do not pretend to be an expert in those fields, but I have gained great insights that have served me well in life.

Think for a moment about your home, your abode, whatever or wherever it is. If you are reading this book at home, you may want to pause for a moment to look around you. How would you describe it? Is it welcoming, elegant, untidy, cluttered, makeshift, grandiose, stark, functional? Realize that what you are looking at is the external manifestation of your inner self. Your outer life, especially your home environment, mirrors your inner self. Also, everything in your home has an effect on you, from the smallest object to the largest design structure.

Unfortunately, most people are not conscious of the huge effect their home and work environments have on them. Many respond unconsciously without even knowing they are being affected. When I was a child, the center of my parental home was the dining room table. Perhaps for others, it was the hearth fire or the kitchen table. Now at this time in our culture, it is the television. If you disagree with me, just observe how the armchairs are arranged in living or family rooms. They are all angled toward the box located in the corner. I am not opposed to television, but it has brought about a lessening in communication and family activities. To compound this problem, there are the cellphones, smartphones, selfies, iPads, computers, etc. These advances in technology accentuate the feelings of separation that many people today feel.

Many of us in the Western world have forgotten what life can be like. We have become separate from the earth, disconnected from our environment, from each other, and from our basic sources of nourishment. Is it any wonder that violence is now rampant in our society? The sacredness of life is lost. When we are out of balance with our surroundings, we are at risk in becoming physically, emotionally, mentally, and spiritually sick. Our lives seem to have little purpose.

At Maria Linden, I created sacred space for myself, but it is much more than that. I am living consciously within the flow of universal energy from which all things manifest. It is about expanding my ability to give and receive love, my capacity for intimacy with people and things, my passion for life itself as my years are now limited.

People enjoy coming to visit in my abode at Maria Linden. Arianne Dawson, the complex manager, uses my apartment as a model for prospective renters, as do the administrators of my religious community. I do not mind the intrusion; I'm always asked in advance. I walk a sacred path: "Everyone helps everyone; everyone is helped by everyone," which fills my life with love and abundance.

Maria Linden is a haven for writers and people who enjoy reading because of the peace, light, harmony, and beauty of the

Sister Barbaralie writing her memoirs in her Maria Linden apartment

apartments, and the tranquility of the entire facility. I use my snack bar, not only for eating, but also as a desk for writing. I'm grateful that I now have the time to reflect on my life. I know that writing memoirs is difficult for a writer at any level. Dissecting my life—deciding what to include and not include, because "my cup runneth over," was a Herculean task. Taking real people, including myself, and turning them into characters, and then deciding about chronology versus thematic organization presented another challenge. And then, I figured out why even accomplished writers scurry away from memoirs and end up fictionalizing everything.

After all of this, I stitched the characters and events together. I was amazed at the emotional responses that surfaced as I wrote about some of my experiences. I found this to be therapeutic and an emotional catharsis. Writing my spiritual journey was not just an exercise. It was prayer. Native Americans have a saying: "When an elder in the tribe dies, a whole library burns to the ground." I was determined not to let my "library burn to the ground."

In all things, wherever we may be, we must learn to welcome the reality and the people the moment brings. These are the people we are living with at this particular moment. For me, this means seniors, some of whom are active, alert, and engaging, while others are having to face limitations. Sooner or later I realize I may be the sister in a wheelchair, or carrying around an oxygen tank, or even bedridden. One cannot live in a place like this and not learn some lessons of life. I'm observing models for my own progressive aging process. It is obvious that every resident, lay and religious, began at a younger age to shape what they are at this stage of life. From their example, I'm asking myself what kind of person do I want to be, and what do I do to fashion that reality? This is the now, and this is where I must learn to live.

The Spirit will give us tomorrow what she wants us to live tomorrow, but wasting time worrying about it is futile. Someone once said, "Worrying does not take away tomorrow's troubles; it takes away your peace." We are all so fragile and vulnerable that we may not even have a tomorrow. We should live the relationship we have with Jesus and His Spirit and with each other now, living in wonderment and trust.

From October 31, 2012 to October 31, 2013, the School Sisters of St. Francis in the United States experienced the deaths of 42 sisters. This was a tremendous loss to our community and to us as individuals who lived, worked and prayed with these deceased sisters. Each death, each loss was a wound to the heart that took us into a period of darkness. Darkness is important. We must be strong and peaceful in darkness, no matter what has caused it, and be still and wait. In accepting this winter of darkness as a gift from God, we will discover that snow will melt and flowers will come forth in all their fragrance and beauty.

Learning to live through the winter is a profound part of any relationship. I believe that no community of people is really born until it has worked through tension and aggression. It is when we have worked through these—whether we are a religious community, husband and wife, or collaborators in work—that we find each other in a new way. Love finds faith and hope only when we have faced pain together, the pain that perhaps is never completely dulled, the pain that is not an impurity, but an essential part of the precious metal of love.

In my life, it is the remembered moments of love that kept me going beyond the limits of my own strength. When love is real, it is powerful in the mark it makes on us. It enlarges and moves us forward. Love's inherent strength makes it more powerful than death, or any of the hazards of life itself. Love is what we Christians should be good at.

In our garden are beautiful trees of many species: oak, linden, maple, pine, cedar, magnolia, crab apple, and others I am unable to identify, but I appreciate their beauty. There is a large cedar tree that attracts my attention through all the seasons. When I stand before the majesty of this tree in summer and autumn, I feel as if the lower, broad branches are going to embrace me. In the winter when it snows, those broad branches catch every flake that falls.

Sister Barbaralie taking a meditation walk in the Maria Linden garden

Thank God for Brother Wind that blows away the accumulation, or many of the branches would break. Thank God for Brother Sun that melts the flakes.

Isn't this what happens to the human soul? The snows of suffering, pain, sorrow, worry accumulate as we reach our limits. Does God really care? Will God intervene and come to our rescue? Is our faith's claim of divine providence real?

There were times in my own life when I was weighed down with pain and sorrow, especially when my sixteen-year-old talented and beautiful niece committed suicide. Only my faith and trust in God and the love and support of friends kept me from breaking. This was a terrible, heart and soul- wrenching experience that tested the faith of my entire family, especially my sister Margaret. The irony is that my niece's name was Faith. Her life, as well as my two-year-old nephew John who drowned, were unfinished symphonies.

Religious fervor increases when one faces death. This is a part of our folklore: "There are no atheists in foxholes." In my particular situation, I can say with certitude, "There are no atheists in retirement homes." It's obvious that when we are older, we see death and become more religious.

Recall what happened to passengers of U.S. Airways flight 149 that made the extraordinary landing in the middle of the Hudson River on January 15, 2009. When the powerless plane descended toward the water, its passengers were faced with the stark reality of death. For many there was a dramatic turn to religion. According to the reports from passenger interviews after the landing, memories included "passengers quietly praying, some reciting the Lord's Prayer, others asking for God's help." From the self-described "not overly religious" to the devout, many had recourse to prayer and religion as they faced dying as a possibility. "I knew I was in God's hands," was one passenger's response. Obviously, turning 80 and 90 are not as dramatic as being alerted by the pilot that the plane is about to have a crash landing.

The *Milwaukee Journal-Sentinel*, November 6, 2013 issue, had an article that captivated my attention: "Art project invites community to fill in the blanks of life." The article written by Mary Louise Schumacher, *Journal Sentinel* art critic stated:

> Death has a way of clarifying life, or so say philosophers and New Orleans artist Candy Chang.
>
> On Tuesday, people in the Bay View neighborhood were confronted by the finiteness of their lives as a result of one of Chang's projects. A wall that reads, 'Before I die I want to …,' and has little buckets of colored chalk so people can fill in the blanks was installed at the Sky High Skateboard Shop and Gallery, 2501 S Howell Ave.
>
> Similar projects were launched in other cities across the United States on Tuesday.

The responses were interesting from people of all ages, "I feel like you have to do things now, before it's too late," wrote a 24 year-old lady who came to the wall to leave her name and response. I don't want to be 75 and in a nursing home and regret the things I didn't do," she continued, and then wrote, "See the world in bright pink."

Another woman of 60 wrote, "Be Reborn" in large letters. By midafternoon, after the wall had been installed, responses included, "give back; become truly happy; learn music theory; be interviewed on Fresh Air." Of course, some inquisitive people came to read what others had to say.

According to Schumacher, "Chang's loss of a friend inspired her to make one of these walls, which has been replicated 350 times in more than 25 languages and in more than 60 countries."

It's gratifying to know that, through the years when we earn the title, "senior citizens," life is seen from a different vantage point. Imagine climbing a mountain. The closer you arrive to the top, the greater the panoramic view. Life takes on a new and different meaning. I now think about God and the world around me much differently than in the formative years of my life as a religious. I have been inspired by scientific teachings of Diamuid O'Murchu, Teilhard de Chardin and the writings of Judy Cannato, Michael Morwood. I have learned that religion and science can be combined to create an expanding view of the universe—an evolutionary faith. After absorbing William Cleary's *Prayers to An Evolutionary God*, I was inspired and even urged to discover my own place in the story of the universe. Donald was a conversion of thinking, too. I was and am challenged to rethink life in new ways and express myself in words that make sense—to an evolutionary God.

Karl Rahner once said that the Christian of the future will be a mystic or nothing at all. W. H. Auden said that prayer "is paying attention to something larger than yourself." What is larger than ourselves? The creativity that dwells at the core of our Cosmos is the largest thing we could ever imagine in this post-Newtonian universe.

What kind of God is an evolutionary God? William Cleary defines it.

> An evolutionary God is the one whose fingerprints and embraces and music we find in the evolutionary patterns in the unfinished world around us, the elusive mother and inventor of this ever-changing milieu. It is a God who pretends—for some purpose we do not comprehend—not even to exist, but whom we can reach out for and give thanks to, if we wish—as most of our race has done throughout its history. …Our evolutionary God is above all a God of desire and love,

of every kind of love we know and of loves we cannot know, a God of colossal wisdom, inventiveness, and risk; a God utterly beyond us, within us, and ahead of us.

Now in my senior years, my prayers are words, songs, and gestures of thanksgiving, praise, and awe.

Correlating with my prayer life is the question: What do I really believe regarding faith as defined by Catholic doctrine? What is Christian, Catholic "faith"? In view of the scientific data about this universe, can we continue to tenaciously cling to a pre-scientific understanding of God, the Cosmos and human origins?

Albert Einstein said, "The important thing is not to stop questioning. Curiosity has its own reason for existing." Therefore, I question and plead for a scholarly, comprehensive study of the origins and relevance of doctrines. I am not a scientist, or a theologian; I am only capable of asking the questions and must look to others for answers. Is it not in our best interest as Catholics to openly and honestly discuss what scriptural scholars and scientists are saying, rather than forcing people to go underground to find a forum for freedom of expression?

Is excommunicating people from office, canonically dismissing priests, and scrutinizing the Leadership Conference of Women Religious a viable way of dealing with a problem that will not go away?

In my wisdom years and as a woman religious who has given 64 years of her life to the Catholic Church, I am deeply concerned about an institutional investment in a closed theology about God and Jesus that is not open to what scriptural scholars and 21st century scientists have to say about the universe. Hasn't the Church learned from its treatment of Galileo and de Chardin? My theology teacher at Alverno College, Father Raymond Parr, taught many years ago: "Theology is not authenticated by conformity to the past, but by relevance to the present."

Holy Spirit of Evolution, Creator of the Cosmos and all its wonders. Thank you for helping us discern the origins and relevance of Catholic doctrines. And for giving us the courage to be open to change. In the final analysis, we trust in you, Silent Mystery, and the evolving plan for us, your pilgrim people and co-creators. We come together in sincerity, openness, and pain, to pool our wisdom, knowledge, research, love, and energies of hope. Convinced that in the end of our struggles, we shall feel the presence of astonishing evolutionary forces at work bringing meaning, direction and promise to your people. We stand at the threshold of time and wait. Amen.

As I conclude my memoirs, I ask myself: In the autumntime of my life, am I still singing the praises of my creative sexuality? How is it applicable or even possible when the passions of youth are no longer as strong and vibrant? Rabbi Abraham Heschel says: "Just to be is a blessing. Just to live is holy." I want to live fully until I die, when I will experience the fullness of life.

The creative energy of my human sexuality is still operative as a celibate. Never have I been more alive. I have learned to delve deeply into the moment with passion and unadulterated sensuousness. I have heightened my awareness and appreciation of the gift of my sexuality and femininity that comes with age.

My energies are directed more fully toward the meaning and sacredness of life and relationships through prayer and contemplation. Life by no means has abandoned me. I savor every moment, especially now since I have the time and space to realize that, without the spring and summer of my life, I could not possibly live the autumntime so fully and enjoy its abundant harvest.

Golden autumn in forest © Olha Rohulya

CPSIA information can be obtained at www.ICGtesting.com
Printed in the USA
LVOW07s2021110914

403616LV00003B/37/P